Karl Leimer   Walter Gieseking

PIANO
TECHNIQUE

consisting of
the two complete books

THE SHORTEST WAY TO PIANISTIC PERFECTION
and
RHYTHMICS, DYNAMICS, PEDAL AND OTHER
PROBLEMS OF PIANO PLAYING

Walter Gieseking
and
Karl Leimer

DOVER PUBLICATIONS, INC.
NEW YORK

This Dover edition, first published in 1972, contains the unabridged text of the following two books:

The Shortest Way to Pianistic Perfection, by Leimer-Gieseking, originally published by the Theodore Presser Co., Bryn Mawr, in 1932.

Rhythmics, Dynamics, Pedal and Other Problems of Piano Playing, by Leimer-Gieseking (translated by Frederick C. Rauser), originally published by the Theodore Presser Co. in 1938.

International Standard Book Number: 0-486-22867-3
Library of Congress Catalog Card Number: 72-82075

Manufactured in the United States of America
Dover Publications, Inc.
180 Varick Street
New York, N. Y. 10014

CONTENTS

THE SHORTEST WAY TO
PIANISTIC PERFECTION

CONTENTS

Walter Gieseking

FOREWORD

The present treatise explains the method of my piano playing, that is, what I consider to be the foundation of my pianistic technique. It is to me a pleasant duty to mention that I owe to Mr. Karl Leimer, under whom I studied from 1912 to 1917, my entire schooling as a pianist. And, now that over twelve years have passed, and after this period of testing, I still am an unconditional partisan of this Leimer method, which I consider the best and most rational kind to bring pianistic possibilities to their highest state of perfection.

Karl Leimer educates the pupil at first to self-control; he shows the pupil how to hear himself. This critical self-hearing is, in my opinion, by far the most important factor in all of music study! Playing for hours without concentrating the thoughts and the ear on each note of the certain study in hand is wasted time! Only trained ears are capable of noticing the fine inexactitudes and unevennesses, the eliminating of which is necessary to a perfect technique. Also, through a continuous self-hearing, the sense for tone beauty and for finest tone shadings can be trained to such a degree that the student will be enabled to play the piano with an irreproachable technique and with a feeling for the sound-beautiful. Really accurately rhythmical playing can be achieved only through severe self-control. How unsatisfying, yes, how unbearable, rhythmically inexact music making is to the listener whose sense of time values, combinations and variations has been highly developed, is indescribable. Unfortunately, and especially in Germany, rhythmically irreproachable playing is seldom heard; and often it even verges on the inartistic. Too much attention is never paid that exact note for note execution of all marks of the composer is the first thing the interpreter should master. I still am grateful to Mr.

5

Leimer that he has trained me to pay unconditional respect to the intentions of the composer. Only the most careful following of all his markings makes it possible to live in the thought and emotional world of a master and thereby to realize a perfect rendition of his works.

In my musical activities I have realized that it is mostly the less gifted musicians, technically and emotionally, who do not fully grasp the content or message of a work and who, because of these limitations, take liberties and retouch a piece in order to make it interesting, which in fact is always a falsification. The young musician almost never understands how difficult it is to play really correctly. That means not only finger-technically but also expression-technically, exactly according to the wishes of the composer. This is possible only by a complete mastery of all kinds of touches and shadings. And this possession must go so far that the musician is able to call up the visionary presentation of a tone or a phrase, in such a way that it automatically transfers itself into the necessary hand and arm movements. The Leimer system, in avoiding all not absolutely necessary movements and in not using all not momentarily needed muscles, and these in relaxation, is undoubtedly the system which carries one quickest to this goal.

It is partly on my insistence that Mr. Leimer has decided to publish these foundation principles of his (or, better, our) system; and I hope that very many pianists will receive much benefit from them.

WALTER GIESEKING.

Hanover, 1930

AN EPOCH-MAKING PEDAGOGICAL ACHIEVEMENT

An Introduction

The late Theodore Presser had unlimited admiration for the teacher who showed in his work real creative and constructive ability. For the teacher who did not think for himself, but merely followed the pedagogical grooves of past decades, he had little respect.

The pronounced progress made in American pianistic methods, by Mason, Mathews and others, was due largely to the fact that these pioneers looked upon the art through spectacles unclouded by arbitrary conventions of the past. Leschetizky, Matthay and Philipp, in Europe, displayed a similar attitude of mind, in that the structures they erected were based upon the past but represented new developments along logical, progressive lines.

During the past few decades the writer has been in intimate contact with the foremost pedagogical methods and materials of the piano and has had frequent conferences with their foremost exponents. This experience has made clear that there is no one supreme method; and the authors of this work display no little audacity in the title, "The Shortest Way to Pianistic Perfection." Still, after reading the work carefully, one must have the impression that it would be difficult to set down a course that would be more direct, more sound and yet more constructive, through its elimination of the unnecessary. Walter Gieseking is recognized by the great pianists of Europe and America as one of the dominating factors in the progress of the art of playing their instrument. Many look upon him as the greatest of the modern school of virtuosi. In this book we have the unusual combination of the methods and practices of the teacher, Karl

7

Leimer, and of his most distinguished pupil, Walter Gieseking. The teacher and the student of pianoforte playing, who make a close study of this very clear and practical work, will unquestionably benefit by a marked improvement in technic and interpretation.

JAMES FRANCIS COOKE

Chapter I

FOUNDATIONS OF MY METHOD

Training of the Musical Ear

Having experienced many fine and exceptional results with my pupils, it has been suggested that I write down my views regarding modern pianoforte playing and thus explain the manner in which I train my students in order to obtain the said success. The following notes lay no claim to completeness; they simply present, in general, the rudiments of my system. A complete insight into my mode of treatment of pianoforte playing could be gained, after all, only through my personal instruction.

My method has brought about a style of execution which differs greatly from the usual piano playing. This method is based upon careful observation and is, I think, perfectly natural; but the way in which I have made use of these principles, and have arranged them into a system, is, according to my experience, the shortest, if not the only way, to develop completely the musical talents of a pupil and to enable him to use the greatest power of expression in his renderings. Doubtless it is only the intelligent and talented pupil who will be able fully to realize and to make complete use of the illimitable possibilities of developing technique and interpretative ability. But my method, with small individual variations, can be generally used; and if rightly understood, it will bring the greatest benefit to every pupil, if he understands how to go to work. Talented pupils obtain results which they would not have thought possi'

If I call my manner of instruction a method
'ly aware that I lay myself open to att'
'wever, I take no notice! My d'
've a polemic character but

forth to general knowledge only what I have recognized, in my long years of practical experience, to be right. The following instructions are not intended for beginners, only for pianists who already have had experience as concert pianists or music teachers, or far-developed, serious-working dilettantes.

The chief point in which my method of teaching differs from that of others, and one of the most important bases upon which it is built, is the training of the ear. Most pianists have not the faculty of hearing themselves correctly. They are accustomed to notice the character of the scales and eventually to recognize wrongly touched tones. But this is not at all sufficient, if one wishes to play perfectly according to our modern ideas. For the pianist the noticing of the exact tone pitch is, so to say, only secondary when compared with the noticing of the exact tone quality, tone duration and tone strength. Through the minute observation of these tonal properties, the whole performance acquires an entirely different clearness and more definite character. In all its separate phases the variable performance will move through a sphere of subtle expression which permits the following of each change and the renouncing of the employment of overly strong dynamic or rhythmical changes. As Gieseking, in his preface, writes, listening to one's self is one of the most important factors of the whole of music study. Nor must one hope to gain this faculty in a day. The capability of listening with a critical ear to one's own playing, and of keeping one's touch under continual control, should be developed systematically by the utmost concentration, as the thorough training of the ear is a prerequisite of rapid progress.

By seemingly pedantically "polishing up" certain parts of a composition, to which but small attention has been given by former masters, a surprising perfection in the rendering of this work can be attained, thus the pupil will be helped to recognize the true character of the piece of music in question. He will discover the many possibilities of improving long studies will not become irksome to him; nor will he lose interest in his work. To all this the master should constantly draw the pupil's attention.

An indispensable necessity, when training the ear, is an accurate knowledge of the piece of music to be studied. It is essential, therefore, before beginning with the practice of the piece, to visualize the same, whereupon, if this has been done thoroughly, we shall be able to play it correctly from memory. To be capable of doing this in a short time, the memory must be specially trained by means of reflection (systematic logical thinking).

It is curious that the method of visualization is not fully and universally utilized. To all my pupils, many of them highly intelligent and talented, and taught by well-known musical instructors, this method has been an absolute novelty. The correct manner of training the memory by means of visualization will be discussed later, but now let us give our attention to Gieseking, who, among all pianists, probably has the largest repertoire and in this many of the most complicated modern compositions. He, however, does not impress these upon his memory (which is looked upon by all musicians as phenomenal) by playing them over on the piano, but by visualizing them through silent reading. By further development of this idea, one acquires the ability even to prepare the technical execution through visualization, so that, without studying at the instrument itself, the piece can be perfectly performed and this in a most astonishingly short time. By many this is thought to be impossible, but in fact it has been done not only by Gieseking but also by other pupils of this method. One pupil was able to memorize in ten to fifteen minutes and to play perfectly and with full expression a piece out of Debussy's "Children's Corner," which he had never seen before. To avoid misunderstanding it might be mentioned that, with the exception of pieces to be publicly performed, specially instructive exercises, and Bach compositions, I do not consider it necessary for the pupil to commit to memory every piece he studies.

Musical instructors, who must themselves have an extensive knowledge of musical literature, should not advise always playing from memory. The brain, however, should be uninterruptedly trained to memorize short phrases. The teacher should insist upon beginners, and even children, learning to play from memory at least one or two measures in every lesson. Such training will bear good fruit! Good results can be, of course, often obtained without doing so; but they cannot be compared to those arrived at by mental study as described above.

In order to attain a natural manner of playing the piano, that is to say, with the least possible strain and exertion, it is of the utmost importance to learn to exert the muscles consciously, and, what is of still greater importance, to relax them consciously. My manner of accomplishing this differs from that of many other pedagogues. I contrive to raise a feeling of relaxation from within, as it were. This is generally attempted by the aid of visible movements. All superfluous movements are injurious. The aim should be the very least possible strain of the muscles when playing the piano.

Chapter II

THE STUDENT BEGINS WORK

(A) A Study from Lebert and Stark

The first thing the pupil must learn is to relax the arm muscles, as is the case when we walk. To attain this I lift the pupil's arm, which should be stretched out at the height of the shoulder but must remain absolutely inert. I then draw away my hand, and the arm must drop down as if dead. In this manner a feeling for relaxing the muscles can be obtained.

The hand has, when one is walking, normally a slight bend; that is, the fingers are slightly curved inwards, which never tires the muscles; whereas the outstretching or continuous greater bending of the fingers somewhat exerts, strains and tires the muscles. The natural position of the hand with relaxed muscles, as is the case when we walk, should be the principal one when playing the piano. When playing, the fingers should be, for the most part, slightly curved, and a pressing through (breaking down) of the knuckle joints should be avoided as far as possible.

The player should sit well forward on the chair, without a support for the back. The upper part of the body should incline slightly forward; the upper arm, bent forward, should hang loosely from the shoulder joint. The seat should be high enough to allow the lifted lower arm to be on a level with the keyboard.

Another important point, in which my playing differs from that usually seen, consists in the elimination of all unnecessary movements. Repose and the avoiding of all unnecessary movements are absolutely necessary, when one intends to play in a decided manner. Any uneasiness endangers not only the tone which is just struck, but also the following ones.

Let us now explain what has been already mentioned, the study of a *simple* composition, and we will choose one of the exercises from the second volume of Lebert's Instruction Book. (See the next page.) The first thing we have to do is to visualize the note-picture, so that the exercise can be written from memory. We take note of the time and key signatures, in this case 2/4 and C major. The right hand commences on the second sixteenth note of the first beat, with the sixth:

Ex.1

Sixths, in sixteenth notes, now descend through two octaves to the tenor

Ex.2

In the third and fourth measures we find an ascending passage of sixths through two octaves from

Ex.3

The fifth and sixth measures are similar to the first and second ones, the only difference being that thirds are inserted in the sixths. Measure seven is like measure three with the third included. The eighth measure brings the sixths of the fourth measure to

Ex.4

14

ETUDE

Lebert and Stark, Piano School

at the last half of the first beat and closes with the
two descending sixths:

Ex.5

    The accompaniment in this case is a broken C
major triad in the left hand. In the first measure a
quarter note C is followed by a quarter rest; and
in the second, third and fourth measures the quarter
notes on E, G and C are followed by corresponding
quarter rests. Measures five to eight are the same
for the left hand as the first four measures. With
the help of visualization, these eight measures can
therefore be played easily, without music; that is,
after careful reading without notes. In the right
hand we find, in the ninth measure, the subdominant
triad

Ex.6

as a quarter note chord, followed by a quarter rest.
In the tenth measure is the same triad, but without
the third,

Ex.7

as a quarter note chord. In the eleventh measure is
the C major triad,

Ex.8

and in the twelfth measure is the same triad without
the third,

16

each quarter note chord followed by a quarter rest. In the ninth and tenth measures, after a sixteenth rest, the left hand begins with a succession of sixths from

Ex.10

through two octaves to

Ex.11

In the thirteenth measure the left hand commences with the next lower sixth,

Ex.12

and the right hand begins two octaves higher with the same chord, followed by a scale passage of sixths ascending through two octaves. In the fifteenth measure the left hand plays

Ex.13

and the right hand, after a sixteenth rest, plays

Ex.14

17

which completes the dominant triad, and it then proceeds in a passage in sixths to

Ex. 15

Measures seventeen to twenty are as the first four were. The four closing measures are similar to the fifth to eighth, an octave higher however, and so altered that the left hand, beginning with the second beat of the twenty-first measure, plays the same unison an octave lower.

By this method of visualization, this careful thinking through of the piece of music in question, the pupil will be capable of writing down the whole exercise from memory. After intense concentration, most of my pupils have been, to their great astonishment, able *in a few minutes of time* to play the entire exercise *from memory.* Visualized reading at the same time affords the pupil the best insight into the form of the composition under study. For instance, the exercise just discussed has been composed in ternary song form. It commences with an eight measure theme, followed by an eight measure middle section, and finally a repetition of the first eight measures in slightly altered form. This easy recognition of the structure of a composition is only one of the many advantages of memorizing by means of visualized reading; and the systematic training of the memory in the above described way permits us to attempt more difficult tasks and teaches us to find out ways and means of facilitating the memorizing of compositions. The pupil with theoretical knowledge of music will soon discover that this, at first somewhat mechanical, process will quickly enable him to grasp the import of a composition.

As a first example a very easy piece has been naturally chosen to show in how far playing from memory can be acquired by visualizing. Our exercise is very appropriate, as it contains a number of important technical problems, which now will be discussed.

The first problem to be mentioned is the touch with the combined upper and lower arm; which, strange to say, is not generally understood. It must, however, be absolutely clear to the pupil, how to do this correctly.

In our exercise the fingers one (thumb) and five, adjusted to play sixths, must be kept motionless, without strain or contraction; and a pressing through of the knuckle joints must be avoided. The position of the fingers should be the same as when, in the act of walking, the arm hangs loosely down from the shoulder joint. The wrist and the lower arm must be brought into position on a level with the keyboard, without strain or exertion. The elbow joint must remain passive, the combined upper and lower arm must be raised from the shoulder only, allowing the first (thumb) and fifth fingers to be lifted about two inches above the keyboard. The hand, which at the same time must be kept under muscular control, is now allowed to drop on the keys, which should be pressed down until "we feel ground," as Rubinstein is supposed to have said. The arm must, as it were, rest on the keys.

These rules are to be taken literally, and they must be carried out to the letter. The above described touch of the "free fall" (as taught by Deppe) is of the utmost importance and is used to render the strongest fortissimo or the softest pianissimo. If the keys are touched every time from the same height, an equal volume of sound for both chord tones is more easily obtained. Moreover, it can be carried out with much greater ease and accuracy, with the combined upper and lower arm, than as if emanating only from the elbow joint or from the wrist.

I would like to emphasize here that, in contrast to many teachers, I very rarely make use of touch from the wrist. It is much more uncertain than the touch just described. Also, by the touch from the wrist, the relaxation of the arm is most difficult to acquire. I am often reproached with causing my pupils to play with a stiff wrist. This is not the case, as the tension of the wrist must be slight and must never be permitted to degenerate into stiffness or cramp.

The left hand tones of the exercise mentioned must be touched in the same manner as the chord tones of the right hand.

As soon as we begin to play this exercise, we commence with training the ear in the following two directions! First, tone quality; and second, tone duration.

Up to the present I have not yet found a single pupil whose ears had been thoroughly trained to hear correctly. None of them were able to distinguish the fine differences in the strength of the separate tones and the difference in the duration of tones. After a period of a fortnight, or even less, however, one and all admitted that they were capable of hearing with completely different ears.

I have found that even most musicians, who believe themselves to have good musical ears, fail in this respect, owing to their sense of hearing not having been trained on these other powers mentioned but only to distinguish pitch of tone. This intensive training of the ear differentiates my system from others. To listen unceasingly to tones as they are played, and to control their accurate execution, is the road that must lead quickly to a polished technique. The fingers are the servitors of the brain, they perform the action the brain commands. If, therefore, by means of a well-trained ear, it is clear to the brain how to execute correctly, the fingers will do their work correctly.

If this is the case and the necessary relaxation is maintained, the fingers in a short time (sometimes immediately, sometimes after a few minutes) will be able to solve the most intricate technical problems. Relaxation is of the very greatest importance. Only by means of the relaxed arm can impulses proceeding from the brain be transformed, without restraint, into finger movements. This is the quickest way to gain control over the fingers. I have seen the most surprising instances and have obtained in a few months results which otherwise could have been gained only by years of study, if ever.

The following is a short summary, as to how my pupils (who in the beginning of their studies should take a lesson daily and later on at least three times a week) would be directed to practice this Lebert-Stark Etude.

First day. The exercise will be played fluently from memory (after visualization), in the manner habitual to the pupil.

Second day. The student will carefully observe:

(1) A correct posture at the piano.

(2) The exact position of the arm and hand.

(3) The posing of the first (thumb) and fifth fingers over the keys of the sixth.

(4) The position of the wrist and elbow.

(5) The lifting and dropping of the entire arm in such a way that the upper arm moves in harmony with the lower arm.

(6) That the keys are touched from a height of about two inches. This may differ, however, as the occasion demands.

(7) That short parts are practiced at a time, and these repeated until perfection is attained.

Third day. The same rules as of the second day will be observed. The feeling of relaxation will be acquired without visible means of help. The pupil must avoid pressing so that the wrist joint breaks down, but he should keep this slightly tense. He should give the most careful attention to relaxation throughout the exercise. If he achieves this aim, he will have made great progress in pianoforte-playing.

Fourth day. An attempt should be made to play the tones in absolute equality of time. Careful note should be taken of the smallest error in this respect, for which a minute training of the ear is indispensable. The more carefully and calmly we attempt this, the sooner we shall see results which are of the greatest importance to technique.

If, after having well considered all that has just been described, we wish to be able in time to play the exercise faultlessly, several weeks of practice and intense concentration will be necessary. The solving of these problems is anything but easy, in fact, very complex; but the intelligent pupil will tackle them with the greatest interest and will have no desire to begin fresh work until he has mastered this first task. Results will be obtained in three or four weeks, through the study of this etude alone, which otherwise would not be reached in months. The pupil now will have become accustomed to a new and natural position of the hand on the keyboard; he will touch the keys with the aid of the entire arm; he will hear the slightest unevenness in the volume and duration of tones; and he will have trained his fingers to obey the brain. Above all, the pupil will have learned to make the strongest demands upon himself and will realize how difficult it is to play, as perfectly as possible, even a simple piece, though written for beginners and children.

In the second week of instruction I show my pupils a different style of touch, which, in my opinion, is the most important one. It is one, however, to which far too little attention is usually given. It is one which, to many, is unknown and will always remain so.

It is of importance that the pupil should make use of this style of touch conscientiously and should become acquainted with the advantages it offers. By its means we can play a beautiful legato, or legatissimo, which does not sound hard and pounded, and we are enabled to produce a "singing" tone. For this style the natural position of the fingers, already described, is of the greatest consequence, because it permits the ample use of the sense of feeling in the finger tips, which is lost if the fingers are too strongly curved inward.

At first the tone should be produced by soft pressure, the first condition being *that the finger does not leave the key at all*—that is, pressure playing is employed. Here again the sense of relaxation in the arm must be retained by the pupil. With the aid of the above described touch, it is possible to render the finest and most delicate shadings. Gieseking's so richly colored rendering of impressionistic music (Debussy, Ravel, and others), which is regarded by musicians and critics all over the world as unexcelled, is due to utilizing fully the possibilities of this style of touch.

(B)   Bach's Invention in C Major

In order to acquaint pupils with the touch just described, the first Two-part Invention by Bach is used. (See next page.) This receives its really correct musical character when thus rendered. The first thing to be done is to visualize the piece, in order that full attention may be given to a legato touch. By the aid of visualization, which at the same time acquaints one with the structure of the composition, it is possible to memorize the piece quickly, if the work is done in the following manner.

First we must again inform ourselves as to time and key signatures—4/4 and C major. The motif begins on the second sixteenth note of the first beat and consists of four tones gradating upwards, and then two descending thirds, ending with a leap to the fifth (dominant). This last leap of a fifth is very frequently altered as the invention progresses. The motif appears literally with the second quarter of the third beat in the lower voice. Hereto are added in the upper voice the eighth notes

Ex.16

as a counterpoint. The first motif is repeated in the second measure, in the upper voice, from G, thus forming

Ex.17

TWO-PART INVENTION

J. S. Bach

with the leap of a fifth to the last note, D. In the same measure the lower voice is approached by a leap from the last note of the previous measure, to the fifth belonging to the motif, followed by another note an octave lower, in counterpoint.

With the second sixteenth note of the third quarter note beat, the motif in the lower voice begins also on G, with the difference that the leap to the fifth has been changed into a leap to the fourth. In the third measure we find inversions of the motif, which are carried out closely four times, the leap to the fifth, however, having been changed every time into an interval of a second. These inversions of the motif follow each other, sequence-like, always beginning from the next lower tone, so that measures three and four can be easily committed to memory, by visualization. In the lower voice we again find four consecutive eighth notes

in counterpoint, then a similar series from G, and finally six scale notes from E. After having carefully studied the notes, the intelligent reader and player will be capable of playing the first four measures of the invention without music. All my pupils are set at this task, which they accomplish without difficulty.

In the fifth measure we find the motif in the lower voice, from D, the last leap having been changed into a leap to the fourth, followed by gradating notes ascending in eighth notes from B to G. The right hand begins with an eighth note A, which drops a fifth to D which leaps a seventh to C; and the measure ends with the motif inverted after beginning with A on the second sixteenth note of the third beat.

In the sixth measure the succession of thirds is continued through the first two beats, to end on fourth line D, after which the cadence to G major closes the first part of the invention. After the pupil has thoroughly visualized these measures and is able to play them in correct time, he can concentrate upon how to learn touch by pressure of the keys.

It is necessary to play the invention very slowly, so as to be able to prepare the touching of each tone and to control every movement. Here again it is of the greatest importance to pay attention to relaxation of the muscles and to even volume of tone, in order to develop the technique of the fingers as correctly and as quickly as possible. It is not advisable to play the whole invention straight through, when studying. In fact, this should be forbidden. Only small parts should be practiced at a time; and these should be repeated over and over again, so that irregularities and unevennesses may be immediately corrected. It is much more difficult, if not impossible, to do this when longer parts are played.

The manner of practicing here presented trains the fingers in a wonderful way, helps the pupil to gain command over them, and eventually leads to perfection in execution.

Grace notes play a very important part in compositions by Bach. There are many players who, when they see these, become frightened and never learn to play them correctly. It is better to use editions of Bach's music in which the grace notes are indicated only by signs over the notes, and not in full notation, as students should be taught to use their own brains. These grace notes, and especially the trill, will later have more detailed attention.

Our Bach Invention affords a good opportunity for learning how to play a mordent, a grace customary in the time of Bach, of which the first principal note is to be taken directly on the beat. The pupil should be shown how very easy it is to play three notes in quick succession (as C, B, C), if the fingers are relaxed, and from the first these notes should be executed as nearly as possible with the same rapidity as it is usual to play a mordent; nor should there be a cessation of study till the execution becomes perfect. Mordents should be practiced with different kinds of fingering. As the first note of a mordent is taken on the first of the beat, it must be struck exactly together with any accompanying principal note taken on the same beat. This must be done with the greatest care and not a moment too early; otherwise inaccurate playing will be the result.

Correct execution will help to train the ear also as regards rhythm. After the mordent has been practiced for some time, the pupil may be allowed to add preceding or following notes. Very often the pupil plays the mordent alone quite correctly. As soon, however, as it is brought into connection with preceding or following notes, there is a slight strain; and in this case it must be practiced again and again, first separately, and then with preceding and following notes. If this method of practicing a mordent is carefully and conscientiously carried out for two or three days, giving special attention to relaxation, the pupil will have learned, once for all, how to play this grace correctly.

The study of this first invention teaches us how to acquire a beautiful "singing" touch through pressure of the keys and absolute relaxation, and how to play a mordent correctly. Even if the pupil does not yet give particular attention to the rendering, but plays the invention in a carefully controlled and even manner, the impression it has made upon him will be greater than if he had played it after his own fashion. These results are gained purely by training the ear and by continual concentration when executing different styles of touch.

It is quite superfluous to play a number of inventions, as the desired results can be gained with more certainty and in a shorter period, if more time is spent on the study of only one or two inventions. All of my pupils showed the greatest interest and endeavored to attain to the greatest perfection in their renderings. One and all realized how quickly they had progressed in technique and felt that such advancement could not have been made by superficially studying a number of inventions.

Phrasing and interpretation will be considered later; but it must be mentioned that not one of my pupils, who had studied the invention in the manner described, had any difficulties in this respect.

(C) Three-part Invention in C Major, by Bach

We will now proceed with the study of the first three part (voice) invention (see next page) which is very instructive. As soon as the pupil has mastered this new task, he will find no difficulty in studying literally the different fugues and preludes of the "Wohltemperirte Klavier."

We must therefore give our very best study to this invention. As a preliminary let us learn, for instance, the repeated touching of the same key, with absolute legato. To accomplish this, the key of the piano must not be allowed to rise to more than three-fourths of its height, so that the tone continues to sound till the key is again pressed down so that the tones become closely linked together. In this manner an absolute legato of two consecutive tones can be played on our modern pianofortes. I also teach my pupils how to glide from one key to the other with the thumb, by means of which a legato can, to a certain extent, be imitated. Another very important matter is the relief of one hand by the other. In most cases the relieving hand is lifted off the keys too soon, so that the tone preceding the relief is not sustained long enough. These inaccuracies, audible only to an attentive listener, lead to a hasty, jerky way of playing, which can be remedied only by training the ear to hear these small, rhythmical irregularities.

Now it must be emphasized that these cardinal mistakes, so often made, can, under many circumstances, completely change the character of a piece. Hence it follows that accurate playing has the greatest influence on correct interpretation. It is an extraordinary thing that this is either unknown, even to many good musicians, or it remains unnoticed by them; and that, to *all* pianists who have

28

THREE-PART INVENTION

J. S. Bach

studied with me, it has meant something absolutely new. Even well-known professionals fall into these inaccuracies, without which they undoubtedly would be still more successful. I therefore attach the very greatest importance to rhythmical accuracy in execution, and am again and again astonished to find how little attention is given to it. People often reproach me with being too pedantic; but these are superficial players, who have not been trained to hear correctly.

To return to the first three-part invention, the first thing to be done is to visualize the notes. We examine the motif and find that it consists of eight tones moving upward by consecutive degrees, followed by three others in the same direction, and finally by four descending downwards. This again appears in the second measure, starting from the keynote; and again in the third measure, starting from the fifth of the key. Each time the beginning is on the second sixteenth note of the first beat of the measure. Having thus carefully visualized several measures, we practice and play them. There are problems to be solved in every measure, which, if they are to be satisfactorily mastered, require careful and concentrated analyzing and practice. It is therefore advisable to tackle one measure at a time, and to continue practicing it until all the difficulties have been overcome.

In the second measure, for instance, attention must be given to the following points:

The legato of the tenor C, must be continued in the second voice, so that the sustained quarter note in the third voice shall receive its value.

There must be a precise relief of the left hand by the right, allowing the tones of the motif to flow smoothly on. The dotted half note, E, in the treble part is to be sustained by the fifth finger, so that it will be connected with the following F-sharp without a break, by passing the fourth finger over the fifth.

In the fourth measure, in going from the F at the end of the first beat to the E on the second beat, the fifth finger must be passed smoothly under the fourth. Finally, care must be given to the legato of the reoccurring E on the last half of the third beat, to be played with the fifth finger. The same execution holds good as regards the repeated A on the third beat and last half of the fourth beat in the second part; in which case the second finger relieves the thumb. Such groups require most careful study. In measure five, the thumb glides from E to D in the second voice, and this must be practiced until a legato of both tones has been attained.

In the sixth measure, E in the third voice must be carefully carried over to the D, by passing the fourth finger over the fifth with a perfect legato. Then there must be a smooth execution of the trill in the treble part.

These brief hints may suffice. It is left to the teacher to show the pupil how to master the above problems in the best and most correct manner, so that he may become fully acquainted with the great advantages to be derived from this invention, if rendered with the utmost technical perfection. It is again emphasized that technique can be increased to a very great extent, if the rendering of compositions be as faultless as possible and, along with this, controlled by intense concentration. Thus we are relieved from the study of many special exercises and become capable of mastering difficulties whenever they appear. In this way we can in a short time learn to control the fingers, which eventually leads to cultivated technique.

It is needless to say that the pupil should be conscious of the fact that illimitable possibilities exist for improvement; and that every time he sits down at the piano to practice he should endeavor to make more perfect the piece he is studying. In most cases, he should in three to four weeks master so well the details that have been discussed that he can commence the study of a Beethoven sonata. Here may be found such an endless store of rich material for study purposes that it seems superfluous to be occupied with an etude at the same time. The numerous scales, trills and other embellishments, along with the many different styles of touch necessary, will, through the thorough study of one sonata, greatly advance interpretation and technique. By carefully observing all indicated shadings, the interest of the pupil is kept constantly awake. If he is fully conscious of the task he has set himself, and if it is his earnest endeavor to make rapid progress, he never will find his studies tedious or irksome.

(D) Sonata in F Minor, Op. 2, No. 1, by Beethoven

As an example we will choose the first Beethoven sonata, the one in F minor. The following suggestions will help to impress it upon the pupil's memory.

The sonata opens with the broken chord of F minor, from middle C to A-flat above the treble staff,

Ex. 19

followed by the notes of a turn on F in the second measure. After this comes the chord of the dominant seventh starting from its fifth, G on the second line, and proceeding to B-flat above the treble staff,

Ex. 20

followed by the notes of a turn on G, and then a repetition of the second and fourth measures. Then comes the F minor chord in the treble, with its fifth highest, and followed by eighth notes in regular scale order downwards to E in the fourth space. The left hand has alternate tonic triads, and chords of the dominant seventh in F minor, which are easy to remember. After having visualized these first

32

eight measures, they can be easily committed to memory, and should be played and practiced by heart.

And right here it might be well to add a few words as regards further perfecting of playing from memory, during the time of study. If we have accustomed ourselves to memorizing such parts by visualization, we little by little develop the capacity of hearing with the "inner ear," when visualizing these parts; and thus we will gradually learn to feel and understand the import of a composition, so that work, which had at first been purely technical, becomes purely mental.

It must be the pupil's ambition to reach gradually these high aims. Only a very few of the elect are born with the talent of immediately and intuitively grasping the meaning of a composition; and they alone have the capability of reaching to so high a degree of mental and manual ability that they can mentally comprehend and correctly render a composition, by means of the fingers, practically without further practice.

In the eight measures already discussed, of the sonata, my pupils are required to play with the combination touch of upper and lower arm, which is altogether much too seldom used. After the staccato notes of the broken chords have been touched, the keys should be released immediately but without a jerk, thus assuring a light and pleasant staccato. This style of staccato touch should be most used; and the sharp, pointed staccato but very rarely.

After the fingers and wrist have been adjusted, the chords of the left hand should be pressed down carefully with the combined upper and lower arm; and care should be taken that "ground" is felt at every tone, so that not one either is missed or gets an undue prominence over the other.

And now we will have just a few words in regard to the interpretation, which of course should be studied only after the technical work is well advanced. The first melody note of the second measure should be slightly emphasized. The triplet begins on the second half of the second beat, precisely. This turn should be played in notes of equal value. The staccato F, the softest tone in the measure, should be shortened by lifting the hand slightly ahead of the full time of the note. The third and fourth measures are to be played like the first and second. The acciaccatura in the fifth measure must be clear. The sforzando must not be taken too vigorously; though it may, however, have more prominence in the following measure. The tones of the broken chord in the seventh measure must follow, in an even volume of sound, one upon the other, the melody tone, upper C, being the strongest. Thorough study and particular care must be given to the four descending tones which follow, each one to be softer than the preceding one.

Here again ear-training and control of the fingers are of the utmost importance. Much can be acquired, in regard to both technique and rendering, if such passages are correctly studied.

The turn in the eighth measure, to which particular attention should be given, is to be played on the first beat, with relaxed fingers and the greatest of evenness. The following E is the softest tone in the measure, and it is taken precisely together with the bass notes. In the left hand the necessary equality of the volume and length of tones is guaranteed by the long lever of the arm.

Attention should be given also to the volume of tone in the different chords. In the ninth measure the left hand should practice the staccato notes of the broken chord, and the following triplet. Most pupils find this difficult, on account of the thumb having to be passed under the fingers. This can be attained by relaxation. In the eleventh measure the tones of the chord C, F, A-flat must be played sharply together, assisted by the combination touch of the upper and lower arm. The staccato notes in this measure must be controlled in respect to correct volume of sound, the first quarter note being slightly louder than the second but standing back in comparison to the triplet.

I should like to point out that triplets are rarely played correctly. They very often create a false impression when heard by trained ears. A rhythmically rendered triplet is a thing unknown to many musicians. In opposition to the intentions of the composer, the triplet is very often not played precisely on the beat. Moreover, it is generally taken too fast and finished too soon. In order, therefore, somewhat to balance the rhythm, the player generally lingers a while before striking the note following the triplet. I therefore go minutely into this matter and insist upon absolute equality in the execution of the three notes. It is only by strictly following this rule that such phrases can be rendered with the right effect. Otherwise, they will always appear uneven and jerky. This may seem pedantic to many, but it is a perfectly natural thing to a musical ear. The correct rendering of triplets is a greater help to technique than is generally supposed.

Measures twelve, thirteen and fourteen of our sonata are to be played like measure eleven. In the middle of the fifteenth measure a slight crescendo is advisable. The G in the following measure, being the end of a phrase, should be played piano, in spite of its appearing on the accented beat of the measure. The thirds in the sixteenth and seventeenth measures for the left hand demand accurate playing together. The octaves in measures eighteen and nineteen for the right hand must be taken as legato as possible. For such passages I prefer the use of the first (thumb) and fifth fingers for the octaves, although large hands can play the treble part perfectly legato by alternating the fifth and fourth fingers on the upper notes. To a trained ear, however, it is distinctly discernible that the sliding of the thumb from one key to another generally disturbs the legato, and it has therefore been found that, with the fingering just given, the octaves can be played more uniformly and more legato. In playing these legato octaves with the first and fifth fingers, each octave should be held as long as possible, and the fingers should glide over to the next only at the

35

very last moment. In this manner it is easy to avoid a side movement of the hand, which generally becomes necessary when the one-five and one-four fingering is employed.

Small hands must necessarily take the first and fifth fingers. Sequences of legato notes, not following in succession, but in large intervals, must be played in the same manner. Each octave must be held as long as possible, the next one following with the greatest rapidity. In studying our sonata, this should be brought to as great perfection as is possible.

In the twentieth measure it is advisable to use "rolling" in the left hand. This rolling is yet another problem to be solved. It can be accomplished either with the combined upper and lower arm from the shoulder joint, or with the lower arm from the elbow joint.

We will here consider the first suggestion and adjust the first and fifth fingers. The rolling movement of the left hand should be practiced until perfect smoothness has been acquired and till both octave tones will have the same power and the entire movement of the hand shall be relaxed and natural. If careful attention is paid to the utmost possible relaxation, the execution will be easy, it will not tire, and it can be carried on for a considerable length of time without fatigue. Rolling from the shoulder joint is to be recommended strongly for pianissimo and fortissimo phrases, for a crescendo from pianissimo to fortissimo, and for a decrescendo. The long lever of the combined upper and lower arm makes an even crescendo and decrescendo possible. The passage in our sonata, necessitating rolling of the hand, can be looked upon as good preparation for tremolos.

In these measures the right hand plays the notes of a chord of the seventh; and they should be rendered legato by pressure of the keys. In the twenty-second measure the notes of the sforzando chord must be struck precisely together; but they must, however, as regards volume of sound, adapt themselves to the piano indicated. Of the end notes

of the phrase, E-flat to A-flat, the last tone principally must be played softly.

In measure twenty-six attention must be given
to the accurate playing together of the eighth notes
in the right hand, with those in the left hand. Moreover strict notice must be given to careful metrical
playing and to a decreasing in sound of the last of
the group of eighth notes in the right hand. The
melody tone, E-flat, in the twenty-eighth measure
must be correctly sustained.

Measures thirty-three and thirty-four afford
an opportunity for studying the F minor scale until
it flows evenly. Here the utmost concentration
must be devoted to equality of length and even
volume of sound for all tones, so that the change
of fingering remains unnoticed. Relaxation should
be impressed upon the mind over and over again.
Measures thirty-seven and forty must be practiced
in like manner.

The difference between the forte and piano
measures must be not too small; these and the accent in the left hand must be distinctly noticeable
to the listener. In measure forty-one the closest
attention must be given to a clear and not too quick
rendering of the acciaccatura and to the correct
value of the eighth note. In these respects errors
often occur. The chords of the left hand in the following measures must be even in length, with their
tones sounded exactly together. It is therefore
necessary to adjust the fingers and to "feel ground."
The fortissimo chord in measure forty-seven should
be played with the combined upper and lower arm,
well adjusted fingers, and the utmost possible relaxation, so that the weight of the arm is thrown
upon the keys. Some players find a difficulty in
accurately connecting the last two chords at the end
of the first part of our sonata. This legato, combined with the different dynamic accents of both
measures, must be conscientiously practiced.

As it is desired to point out only in general the
way I go to work, when commencing the study of
a composition, these suggestions may suffice in

respect to the first section of our sonata movement. And now we will consider briefly the second movement.

The second movement begins with an incomplete measure on middle C, which should be played more softly than the first A of the next measure. In the incomplete measure the sixteenth note must receive its full value but must be played slightly softer than the preceding note. The melody tone, A, at the beginning of the first full measure, should be well emphasized. The musical term, "p," is in force throughout the whole part. The turn should be played with absolute evenness as regards the value of the notes, softer than the melody tone, A, has been, and this with relaxed fingers. The grace note, C, is taken precisely on the second beat, exactly with the D-flat of the left hand. The eighth notes, B-flat, A, G, F, being melody tones, must dominate the accompanying notes; they should not be of even strength but should gradually decrease in volume of sound. Again the melody tone, F, in the second measure should be taken slightly louder, with the following E legato and much softer. In pronouncing the word "solo," we put the accent on the first syllable, "so," letting the second syllable, "lo," drop away; the same applies to the two just mentioned tones.

The accompaniment in the left hand must be considerably subdued. In these three part measures, are, therefore, three different degrees of tone volume to be observed; the melody slightly louder than piano, the lower notes piano, and the middle voice still more softly. The middle part tones should be played like the treble part tones, decreasing (very slightly) in sound towards the end of the measure. In the beginning of the second measure the relation of the volume of sound of the different parts is the same as in the first measure. The notes, from the middle of the second measure, should slightly increase in volume to the melody F in the third measure, which latter must be brought into prominence. The melody C, at the second half of the first beat of the third measure, should have less of power, and the finger should be lifted off the key slightly before the usual length of the note. The same holds good for the second and third beats, with a decrease of sound at the end.

The fourth measure should be played like the second. The lower thirds must be quite subdued. The relation of the left hand chord notes to each other is the same as in the preceding measures. In regard to the end notes of the fourth measure, a slight crescendo to A in the fifth measure should be made. The crescendo of the sixth measure may be fairly strong, so that the sixteenth notes in the right hand shall have the effect of a song.

The performance of these first measures, with the illustrated natural rendering just outlined, is very difficult and requires a very critical ear. If correctly played the pupil will learn a considerable amount, as regards both ear and technique, as thorough control of the fingers is essential if the mentioned problems are to be solved correctly. It has been already mentioned how greatly technique can be perfected. By the study of these small parts as described, the use of many an etude will be made superfluous.

The thirds for the left hand, in the seventeenth measure of the second movement, must be quite subordinate to the melody tones and must be played precisely together. The last third of each group should be the softest but must receive the same time value as the preceding ones.

The eighth notes in the twenty-seventh measure are often hurried. These tones demand a decrease in volume of sound, but can, however on the other hand, be played crescendo, in order to prepare the sforzando in the beginning of the following measure. These eighth notes should be played louder than the preceding pianissimo tones. I suggest mezzopiano.

The overlapping triplets in the twenty-ninth measure must be carefully practiced. We come across a difficulty in this measure. The second note of the triplet in the right hand must be unaccented, whereas the left hand at the same time begins with a slightly accented sixteenth note and adds a third sixteenth note softly. The hands must be independent of each other. In this case the unaccented right hand must be played together with the somewhat accented left hand. To master this difficulty, the utmost concentration, slow practicing, and at first strong exaggeration of the accents, for both the right and the left hand, are necessary. One hand must relieve the other rhythmically and precisely, and the ear must listen carefully. Great progress in technique can be made if such difficulties are mastered successfully. Measure thirty-six will now cause no difficulty.

In measure thirty-seven the difficulty is to play three notes in the left hand against four notes in the right. A preliminary exercise is necessary in this case. The left hand should play the six notes of the last beat several times slowly, the player counting aloud the half-beats or eighth note values. After this has been repeatedly done, the right hand should immediately, and without a break, play over and over the thirty-second notes in the treble, in the same way.

The pupil must count half-beat groups loudly and uninterruptedly, and the right and left hands should follow each other evenly. It is absolutely necessary to take the triplets evenly and then to follow these with the groups of four thirty-seconds in the same time spaces, in order to accustom the ear to the different durations of the sixteenth note triplets and the thirty-second note groups. It is advisable to make use of a metronome. As soon as we are able to play three and four notes in time to the half beats, we practice the right and left hand alternately three or four times, and then at once try both hands together, without, however, interrupting the rhythm, and all the time listening carefully first to one hand and then to the other. Again and again we return to playing the hands separately, until an accurate rendering of both hands together has been attained. When we have fully solved this problem, and one hand is independent of the other, we find that we have made great progress in technique. The sixth measure before the end of the movement is generally taken too slowly, and here attention must be given to correct time.

The melody tones in the beginning of the third movement of the sonata (A-flat, B-flat, G) must have greater volume than the lower sixths belonging to them. These sixths, and the many nuances necessary in the rendering, are problems not easy to solve. The first beat B-flat must sound louder in tone than the incomplete measure; and G must be subdued. Prominence must be given to the melody tones of the four-note chords in the third measure, and these must be played legato, with the middle parts subdued. The C in the alto, occurring five times, must be played legato and very carefully. The thirds in the bass also must be very subdued, and they must be played precisely together with the other chord tones. The melody B-flat in the fourth measure should be slightly emphasized; and the A-flat should, as regards volume of sound, resemble the softly spoken last syllable of a word. The pupil will benefit greatly, if he studies these four measures thoroughly.

In the fifteenth and following measures we again find the hands relieving each other, as described heretofore, with alternate accents. Special attention must be paid to the legato of the fortissimo chords in their first inversion, in the Trio, which is very difficult; and attention should be given to an even rendering of the crescendo and decrescendo.

In the last movement (prestissimo) the chords calling for the five fingers of the right hand must be touched with special strength, thereby producing a clearer sound. The arpeggios in the bass demand equality of tone, which becomes even more difficult when the chords extend over two octaves.

Here we find again good materials for scale study. The playing together of even eighth notes against triplets of eighths, at measures twenty-six to twenty-nine, and of which the pairs for the left hand again must be played with the "rolling" movements, serves to fix the smooth playing of passages of two even notes against triplets. The last movement offers no new problems, but it affords the opportunity of developing the fingers in a manner which no special etude could furnish. The execution of the octaves with first and fifth fingers, and the flow of the cantilenas, the chord accompaniment in the left hand, and so on, have just been discussed.

In playing this sonata we realize how wonderfully instructive it is and how great the profit we can gain by studying it thoroughly. It is well worth spending some time in doing so. The intelligent pupil, as he realizes how much he can gain technically, and as he becomes familiar with the character of the composition, will not lose interest in it. On the contrary, it will be his ardent endeavor to attain to the highest perfection in both technique and interpretation, and his pleasure in doing this will continue to grow.

Chapter III

NATURAL INTERPRETATION

Let us now for a short time consider natural interpretation. The pianist very often believes he must alter the musical notation of a composition, especially as regards rhythm. He very often does so unconsciously, because he is not capable of reading correctly, because his playing is superficial, or because he thinks it is more interesting and "expressive" to play, let us say, a succession of sixteenth notes unevenly and strongly rubato, although the composer has written them all of equal value. Many of the audience may applaud such distortions, but the most distinguished and most renowned musicians are very particular as to accuracy in their interpretations and reject all that is contrary to the intentions of the composer. *Absolutely correct execution* of a composition is the only foundation upon which a really excellent interpretation can be built.

It would certainly go too far and irritate the player, if the composer were to write down fully the terms necessary to all his minor interpretative intentions. There are certain aesthetic rules of rhythm, style and form, which the musician must know and feel. We must accordingly feel where a slight accelerando or ritardando is permitted or relevant.

We will now occupy ourselves with the principal features of phrasing and unusual accents which imply no unevenness of tones, but a proportionately slight ritardando or accelerando. It is a well-known fact that every phrase has its climax, to reach which a slight hurrying of pace, or a slight increase of sound is permitted, whilst the reverse should take place from the climax to the end of the phrase. If these fine points, therefore, are executed in the right manner, that is to say, in natural proportion, they

43

will doubtlessly serve to vitalize the phrase, will correspond to natural musical feeling, and will increase expression.

It need not be mentioned that care must be taken not to overdo these changes of tempo. The pupil must be trained to feel what is correct, and the teacher should indefatigably point out to him how to modify rhythmical tempo proportionally, and should not pass over lightly anything in this respect. In order to attain to a natural and perfect manner of execution, it is essential to master thoroughly all technical features of a composition. After visualization and thought have shown us which tones should be accented, where an increase or decrease in sound or in pace is correct, and when we have done complete justice to all this technically, we will find that our power of expression has become greatly influenced and that we have learned to feel with greater warmth.

When I have said to my pupils: "I will increase and animate your powers of feeling," they at first have shaken their heads, but afterwards enthusiastically admitted the truth of my prophecy. I quote this because many people assert that in music feeling must predominate over the brain. In my opinion, however, a convincing interpretation can be acquired only when both are combined. Inaccurate and disproportionate interpretations of crescendo, diminuendo, ritardando, accelerando, against which Hans von Bülow so passionately declaimed, take away from the naturalness of the interpretation and gravely injure the pupil's musical taste. These injuries are facts, which most music pedagogues fail to realize.

Inaccuracy and uncertainty in rhythm and dynamic feeling become so firmly fixed in the brain, that, as has been already pointed out, they can be mended only with great loss of time, if ever.

Execution is dependent upon a correct style of touch, and it is advisable to execute certain passages with a certain touch. If the pupil, therefore, wishes to discover the easiest, most accurate, and the most tasteful manner of execution, it is essential for the teacher to be or to have been a good pianist, so that he knows the advantages and has control himself of the different styles of touch. Many seemingly very difficult, and to all appearances unplayable, passages are sometimes easily mastered if, after careful reflection, the correct touch is used.

In many cases, of course, opinions of professionals differ, in regard to correct execution. It is possible that the musical terms dictated by the composer are felt to be insufficient, but they undoubtedly help in finding out the correct way in which the composer wished his works to be interpreted. I, myself, have found that there are not so many disputable interpretations, and that the opinions of musicians with a natural sense of feeling do not vary so greatly. I have nearly always succeeded in convincing my pupils of the way in which they should render the pieces they were studying. When they played them according to my instructions, they did so with so much warmth and intensity of feeling that I had the impression "they feel the same as I do." It was not their verbal agreement that convinced me but their musical interpretation. With the aid of numerous examples, I have caused my pupils to learn the relative strength of a tone in relation to other tones and have found them agreeing with what I felt to be correct. I look upon this as a proof of the accuracy of my interpretation.

Chapter IV

MAKING STUDY COUNT

A remedy, which is sometimes very effective in convincing the pupil, is to sing small parts to him. In order to be able to execute any part of a composition correctly, it is in the first place necessary to consider its musical import, and to know where the climax is; in the second place, to master it technically, so that the player is in a position to express what he feels without a hindrance.

It may be well, right here, to say a few words about practicing, and to point out the quickest way to reach the desired aim, and what will lead to the greatest possible perfection. One of the most important duties of a pedagogue, if not *the* most important, is to teach the pupil how to practice correctly. He deserves the greatest praise if he untiringly points out to the pupil the best way to work.

Most teachers have their pupils to practice their pieces for too short a time, and then go on to something new before the work in hand has been thoroughly mastered. In opposition to this, and from the results of long years of experience, I maintain that the greatest progress, both technically and musically, is made from that moment when the teacher usually gives the pupil a new piece although in regard to the old piece there is still much of the greatest importance to learn. Teachers do this because they fear the pupil's interest might lag, while they overlook the fact that it is through a minute and careful perfecting of all parts of a composition that the greatest profits are gained and that real progress is assured.

It is when most people think that they have "finished" the study of a certain piece that the most important work begins, namely, to train the ear.

Now that the pupil has learned how to work out details, he experiences the greatest interest in his studies, and he realizes how illimitable are the possibilities of improving and progressing. The niceties of the composition become familiar to him, his musical studies are a joy, and he becomes more sure of his own capabilities, so that he loses practically all feeling of nervousness when on the concert platform.

Practicing signifies the continual repetition of some part of a piece, and has the following effect:

When a part of a composition has been played for the first time, a picture of the same becomes imprinted on the brain. This picture varies in clearness according to the mental constitution of the pupil. In general, a very faint impression is left on the memory, similar to a photograph which is not clear or has been under-exposed. Through constant repetition the picture becomes more and more distinct and finally resembles a clear, sharp photograph.

The mistakes made, when playing, again cause a picture to appear in the brain, which, however, being faulty, needs correction. This is very often a most difficult and wearisome business; and faults, especially in regard to rhythm, and acquired through incorrect practicing, can be eradicated only by great effort. For a pupil, therefore, who wishes to make quick progress, it is of the greatest importance to avoid mistakes, from the very beginning. This can be attained, in the first instance, by playing very slowly, by thorough concentration in regard to rhythm (I would suggest counting aloud), and by the use of correct fingering. By means of absolute concentration the pupil is generally able to play small parts absolutely correctly, in the course of a few minutes; this being otherwise, very often, only possible after days or weeks of study.

As has been already mentioned, I think it harmful to pay attention to the interpretation of a piece while it is being studied, as the pupil is at first too much taken up with technical problems. If the interpretation is incorrect, a false impression is made

47

upon the ear of the pupil, and the tiring business of correcting mistakes has to begin all over again. The pupil should first study a small part thoroughly, and then he should go on a bit farther (it is not necessary to play to the end of a phrase) and practice this in exactly the same manner. Three or four short parts may be now practiced together.

The objection that it is better to practice only complete phrases, instead of dividing them up, does not hold good. The way that has been suggested is not in the least harmful to musical feeling. On the contrary, the thorough mastering of short parts of a phrase at a time will enable the pupil to bring the complete phrase to a state of greater perfection.

The uninterrupted concentration of from twenty to thirty minutes will probably tire the pupil. It is then useless to continue practicing, as results thus gained are not worth mentioning. In the beginning, therefore, I forbid my pupils to practice longer than the given time, as their attention is likely to wander, so that further work becomes harmful rather than helpful.

After having practiced a short time, the pupil should pause for a while, in order to allow the brain to rest, and then commence work again in about an hour's time, beginning with the phrases he had last practiced. It is sufficient even for concert players to practice one-half an hour five or six times a day. To practice the piano five, six, or seven hours daily is generally done without concentration and is at the same time injurious to the health. The mental study demanded by the method here outlined is naturally very strenuous, and pupils afflicted with mental inertness greatly dislike it. But it is the only way in which really good and astonishing results can be obtained.

Every piano pedagogue asserts, however, that he demands mental study; but it is quite astonishing in how small a degree this is really carried out. Among the hundreds of pupils with whom I have come in contact, many of whom were highly intelligent and talented and had studied with renowned pedagogues, I did not find a single one who could in the slightest way use his brain correctly when practicing. When pupils assert that they make use of mental study, it is usually only talk. Untiring patience on the part of the teacher is essential, in order to force the pupil himself to concentrate. As has been already said, this is the foundation upon which to build up playing from memory.

Chapter V

SPECIAL TECHNICAL PROBLEMS

(A)   Etudes

To acquire good technique is also mental work. If this intensive work is done by the help of strong concentration, it is possible for technique to improve so rapidly that marvelous results will be sometimes obtained. Almost always, however, brain work is left out, and the pupil is obliged to spend many years of practicing daily, and for hours at a time, in order to acquire a somewhat serviceable technique.

I am not absolutely opposed to finger exercises, scales, and arpeggios, nor do I reject the study of etudes; but I am of the opinion that these means for developing technique are, as a rule, used too much. To sit at the piano and practice scales and exercises for hours and hours, generally without concentration, is a very roundabout way of obtaining results. It is pernicious to the health and mind of the pupil and very often causes a nervous breakdown, either before or after the examination which all the students studying at a college of music are nowadays obliged to pass.

I allow my pupils to play only a very few etudes, but demand that these be brought to the utmost possible perfection. The assertion that it is essential for the teacher to be well informed as to the etude materials such as Heller, Bertini, Cramer, Clementi, Moscheles, and so on, is partly justified; but an acquaintance with these should be gained largely through their use for the purposes of sight playing. Playing at sight is of the very greatest importance and should help the student to a wide acquaintance with good music. Thorough study should, however, be applied only to some specially instructive etudes; and this should be done in the intensive way pointed out when discussing the short etude in the beginning of this treatise. A small number of thoroughly studied etudes will suffice to develop good technique, which, by proper methods of study, can be acquired in an astonishingly short time; whereas the use of many etudes brings only slow progress, wastes the student's time and ruins the nerves.

There are many, however, who object to my stand on this subject and say that an extensive study of etudes is necessary, on account of many of them being masterly works. That may be true, but the studying of too many etudes is undertaken at the expense of our classical masters, when they should be regarded as only preparatory for the latter. It seems to me to be of greater importance that the time at our disposal should be applied to the study of as many classical works as possible, such as sonatas by Beethoven, Mozart, Haydn, Schubert, and so forth; and with these also chamber music and orchestral works should be studied. Everybody will admit that such musical compositions are of higher value than even the best etudes, and that an accurate study of these works will afford a much better insight into the individuality of the composer, thus creating in the player an ever growing enthusiasm for the same.

The teacher must understand how to draw the pupil's attention to the beauties of the works of our classical composers, and he can do this only if he is himself capable of valuing and appreciating them. Most pianists are far too little acquainted, both with the compositions of good composers and with musical literature in general. My hints in regard to practicing will probably be new to many people. They differ widely from the usual method and conception of teaching.

(B)   Playing of Scales

To a certain extent, of course, the practicing of finger exercises and scales cannot be avoided, and it is well therefore to make a few further remarks, which I think will be advantageous when studying. Here again the ear plays a most important part.

It is a grave mistake, and one which is frequently made, to allow both hands to play together when practicing scales. Scales are played with a view to training the fingers, so that they do their work evenly and smoothly. Every tone of a scale must be struck with a certain vigor, and the ear must be carefully trained to hear the exact volume of sound required. We must have an accurate knowledge of the notes appearing in the scale, in order to be able to play it from memory; and we must further acquaint ourselves with the fingering, that is, the use of the thumbs and the third and fourth fingers. Not before the notes and the fingering are familiar to the pupil should he begin playing.

As the ear must pass judgment on the correct volume of sound, it is the first condition, when playing scales, for each hand to practice alone. If this is not done, the left hand is drowned by the right hand, or *vice versa;* for it becomes almost impossible to find out the grade of strength of the different tones with the two hands playing together.

In the scale of C major, for instance, C in the left hand is played with the fifth finger, in the right hand with the thumb; D in the left hand with the fourth finger, in the right hand with the second finger; and so forth. As the fingers are unequal in strength, they cannot at first be expected to touch the keys evenly. It is almost impossible for the beginner to hear these dissimilarities, if both hands are played together.

The most important thing when training the fingers (the control of which we call technique) is to be able to judge correctly of the dynamic value of the tones, by means of the ear. One must, therefore, bear in mind that the tones of a scale must be played with equality of strength. For the thumb there must be an extra pressure; for the second and third fingers there will be a certain amount of restraint; and then again for the fourth and fifth fingers there will be an added strength of stroke. Strange to say, it is little known that in many cases the thumb touches the keys too feebly, a sure sign of how imperfectly the ear is generally trained. The movement, which comes naturally to the thumb, is to bend it under the other fingers, whereas the striking of a key from above downwards necessitates practice and will be found not so easy. Although the thumb may be looked upon as the strongest finger, it as a rule strikes the keys too feebly. Its position, by reason of its being somewhat closer to the keys than the other fingers, encourages a weaker playing. For the same reason the thumb very often strikes too feebly when bent under the fingers, and on the other hand too vigorously, either through want of relaxation or through clumsiness.

After the thumb has been bent under, attention must be given to the second finger and, in descending, to the third and fourth fingers. Only by playing very slowly can we assure ourselves of the dynamic value of each tone, which is necessary in order to discover and to correct inaccuracies of equality in power. The best and quickest way to do this is to play short passages of the scale, and to practice five tones ascending and descending. The most careful attention must be given to the rhythm and touch of every tone. Rigid concentration guarantees control of the fingers and leads to success.

Having taken note of the volume and the rhythmical value of tone, attention must be given to movement of the muscles. The feeling for absolute relaxation must become second nature to the pupil, and it must be continuously felt when playing scales. If the player gives constant attention to these three points, keeping watch over both hands, and practicing a short time every day, he in a few weeks will have acquired so great a technique that he will be able to play scales in a much better manner than many pupils who have been studying for years and have practiced scales one hour or more a day. If the pupil follows these rules, his playing will become smooth and rippling. Naturally the hands should be occasionally practiced together, in order to accustom the ear to the precise striking together of the tones of the two hands.

A great difficulty when playing scales is the passing over and under of the fingers. We must think ceaselessly of relaxation. I advise the passing under of the fingers to be practiced principally by rolling of the lower arm; whereas this is usually done by a side movement of the hand over the keyboard. It is, moreover, quite easy to relax the muscles when using a rolling of the lower arm; and this is difficult when the hand is bent sideways.

Without relaxation it is quite impossible to play a pearly scale. After having touched a black key, it is comparatively easy to pass the finger under; but this is not so, however, after having touched a white key. For this reason the scale in C major is the most difficult to play smoothly. It is therefore advisable not to commence with the C major scale. At a later period, however, it is the most suitable one for practicing.

I attach so great an importance to finished scale playing that I should like to repeat the principal rules to be observed when studying the same:

In the first place practice should be slow, in order to allow control of the evenness of the duration of tone and of the volume of sound.

Small parts should be practiced at a time, until they can be rendered to perfection.

There should be the greatest possible relaxation, a natural position of the fingers, as already described, and a rolling of the lower arm when passing the fingers over or under.

Side movements should be avoided as much as possible.

When descending, there should be a swinging over the fixed and outstretched thumb. The thumb should glide over the keys; and it should be somewhat extended, for if it is bent in the first joint it is likely to knock against the protruding keys.

All the twenty-six scales should be studied; which is to say, the pupil should be conversant with their key-signatures and fingering and should be capable of playing them at a certain pace. I do not consider it necessary to play scales in all their variations of sixths, thirds, contrary motions, and so on, as too much valuable time is wasted thereby. It cannot much harm the pupil to practice these variations; but it is a strain on the nerves and takes up time which could be better employed. Scales or parts of scales, however, as they constantly appear in compositions, should be carefully studied, so that in time their rendering will, with the help of relaxation, become more and more perfect.

(C) Broken Chords

Broken chords should be played in a manner similar to scales. When passing the fingers under or over, the rolling movement should come in evidence. The fall of the hand on the keys helps to balance the fingers. An even touch is somewhat more difficult when playing arpeggios than when playing scales, as the consecutive tones lie farther apart. Under no circumstances, however, may the fourth finger be spared. Many pupils try this by using the stronger third finger. Apart from the fact that by so doing the position of the hand is somewhat strained, the fourth finger will not develop sufficiently; and, as it is the weakest of the five fingers, it needs special care and attention. It is good practice to use the fourth finger in place of the third. With a few exceptions, the third of the arpeggio in the left hand should be always played with the fourth finger.

The study of arpeggios of the dominant seventh and diminished seventh chords is of the greatest benefit. All the fingers are used; and moreover it is much more difficult to relax, as far as possible, not only those muscles which are brought into action but also those which are not, as the stretch required for arpeggios is considerably greater than when playing scales. Relaxation will produce a smooth and even execution; and with the help of a well trained ear, absolute equality of tone can be attained.

(D)   Playing Chords

A faulty and uneven rendering of chords is an error very often committed, even by well known concert pianists. How often in our concert halls we hear pianists neglecting to sound their two hands exactly together. It is remarkable that even amateurs criticize an orchestra, if chords are not played precisely together; whereas on the concert platform this grievous offense against all musical feeling is nearly always overlooked. Both hands must strike the keys precisely at the same moment. This may not be easy, but it is a means of enormous importance to expression; and the concert player would do well to study it thoroughly.

Attention should be given to the different degrees of strength with which the separate tones of a chord are played with one hand. The most important finishing touches of a performance are accomplished through the mastery of this element in piano technique. This is most difficult and its accomplishment demands the utmost concentration and diligence. It will, however, on the other hand, be found most interesting.

It is extremely difficult to render a melody with expression, if both melody and accompanying chord tones are played with the same hand. Apart from the fact that the melody tone should be two or three degrees stronger in sound than the accompanying tones, it must adapt itself in sound to the preceding or following tones. The chord tones should not drown the melody tone, nor should one of them be played too feebly or be missed. They must, as it were, serve as a background to the melody tones, which should stand out like bright shining lights. Needless to say that perfect technique and absolute control of the fingers are necessary, and these can be obtained only by carefully training the ear. The effects Gieseking produces in this respect are wonderful.

It is remarkable that the relation of the melody tones to the tones of the accompaniment is more or less absolute, and that my pupils felt the correctness of dynamic accent in the same passages as I did.

(E) The Trill

As regards graces, the mordent and the turn have been already mentioned. The most important one, however, and the one most often occurring, is the shake or trill, about which a few words should now be given.

The acquiring of a round and even trill is to a very great extent dependent on the ear and on the relaxation of the muscles. Most students find the trill very difficult to play, and as a rule it takes the pianist many years before he can successfully accomplish it. Concentration, however, works wonders. Some of my pupils have played a trill smoothly and evenly in the course of a few weeks, in spite of their first attempts having been clumsy and awkward. The secret of this is, as has been already said, in keeping one's ears open and in paying careful attention that the alternate tones of the trill follow in exact time one upon the other, neither too quickly nor too slowly.

If the student keeps constantly in mind that the muscles must be relaxed, and if he practices the trill daily eight to ten times, he will undoubtedly reach his goal. If, however, he does not succeed in this, he does not understand how to regulate his fingers by means of careful listening to his playing, or he either forgets to relax the muscles or has no control over them. Whoever follows the method here advised may expect certain success.

It is naturally necessary to study every possible fingering for the trill, especially with the third and fourth fingers, through which the weakness of the fourth finger will be improved to the fullest extent. The turn at the end of the trill, if played with the second finger, does not demand a motion of the hand, as is very often the case when the thumb is used.

Many players find a difficulty in keeping the fingers on the keys while playing a trill. This, however, adds greatly to a fine execution of the trill; as the sensitive nerves in the fingertips play a very important part in the position of the fingers described above. I do not recommend the practice of special trill exercises, but do have my pupils to study thoroughly, for instance, the *Sarabande* from Bach's "French Suite in E major," by means of which most of my pupils acquire a faultless trill. This enables them to play the *Sarabande* to such perfection that they feel themselves amply repaid for the strenuous mental work they had to undergo. To discuss further the different kinds of trill, the fingering, and so on, is unnecessary.

(F) Tranquility in Movement

Before closing this treatise on my system of pianoforte teaching, I should like to mention one further point, in which the pianists I have trained differ in general from others.

All unnecessary movements should be avoided. During a lesson I again and again draw the pupil's attention to the fact that both fingers and hands should be kept as near to the keyboard as possible, in order to insure certainty of touch. This means, however, not only certainty of striking the right key but also certainty as regards quality of touch, which is best assured if the fingers are allowed to lie on the keys.

Once the key has been struck, nothing can be done to change the quality of the tone, nor can a motion of the arm, hand or body have the slightest influence upon it. Most pianists make use of striking movements of the body and arms, thinking thereby to impress the spectators. These movements have, as already mentioned, absolutely no influence, either on the tone already struck or on those to follow.

The careful playing of a tone with a certain strength is usually possible only by carefully touching the keys; and to do this necessitates calmness and control of the nerves. In many cases certain movements before striking the keys cannot be avoided; but they should be restricted so far as to guarantee quality of tone, which must not seem as if left to chance. It is of course possible to play even when moving the body about, and many people do this to a great extent; but the highest measure of certainty in execution can be guaranteed only by keeping the body quiet. It has been already pointed out that one can relax the muscles without motion, therefore the movements many pedagogues advise their pupils to make, in order to learn how to relax, are superfluous.

The work the pianist has to accomplish is by no means easy; and, needless to say, it should not be rendered still more difficult by unnecessary and superfluous movements! Moreover, it should become second nature to the pianist to avoid everything that does not agree with the intentions of the composer. It should be his principal aim to acquire so perfect a style of execution as to enable him to recreate the beauties of our great composers' works. The player, who has trained his ear by means of the strictest concentration, to hear and to feel every nicety in interpretation and technical execution, will be foremost in achieving these. By unceasingly listening with "the inner ear," as it were, to a composition, his capability of comprehending it will develop to so great an extent that he finally will grasp it in all its details and will be in a position to interpret this master work in its greatest perfection.

Sonate Nº 1.

65

MENUETTO.
Allegretto.

Trio.
a tempo

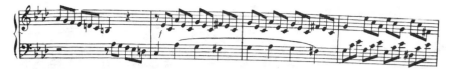

INDEX

75

RHYTHMICS, DYNAMICS, PEDAL AND OTHER PROBLEMS OF PIANO PLAYING

CONTENTS

PREFACE

My book, "The Shortest Way to Pianistic Perfection," written in collaboration with Walter Gieseking, has found a vast circulation at home and abroad and has won spontaneous approval almost without exception. I have received many requests to publish supplements thereto.

This second book occupies itself almost exclusively with the education of concert pianists and gives instructions to pedagogues, who guide their pupils until they have reached artistic maturity. I have often been questioned as to how far these suggestions can be applied to beginners, college students, and serious-minded amateurs.

These aforesaid suggestions for pianists are indeed just as practical for primary instruction and also for players of other instruments. Because of repeated invitations, I then published the lectures which I gave at the Municipal Conservatory in Hannover (whose founder I am) in the form of the present supplementary volume to "The Shortest Way to Pianistic Perfection." The material for these lectures came through my own pedagogical experience and was compiled from different sources.

In this supplementary volume a thorough discussion with regard to questions on Rhythmics, Dynamics, Modes of Touch, and Phrasing takes place. A separate chapter was devoted to the Use of Pedals, since very little material on this particular subject is available. I deem that these very applications are exceedingly important, since the application of the pedal is difficult to teach.

Many questions arise again and again with regard to the present applications, although they have formerly been discussed, of course, from a different point of view. But this is immensely important with regard to instruction, because many things cannot be repeated often enough: *Repetitio est mater studiorum.*

The chapters on reflection and technique through mental work have been inserted, since these problems are generally treated too carelessly, in spite of their importance.

Hannover, December, 1937.

KARL LEIMER

I. INTRODUCTION AND REFLECTION FOR THE MENTAL CONCEPTION OF THE ALLEMANDE FROM THE FRENCH SUITE IN E MAJOR BY BACH

It is an important pedagogical experience to confine oneself to a single problem while studying a composition if the single tasks are to be understood thoroughly and carried out in all details. However, more advanced pupils will be able to treat more than one problem at the same time when practicing. This is an asset to their future success.

One should first of all concern himself with the impression of notation and acquaint himself with the valuation of notes. After mastering these rudiments, one should learn the proper modes of touch. One thinks of composite rendition only after the preceding problems have been satisfactorily solved. First-class piano playing is possible and thinkable only after these problems have been rendered exactly and with utmost care. This successive solving of problems, which must also be a matter of utter concentration, is not the only ways and means for reaching a goal, inasmuch as we also learn to see and understand them in the quickest and best manner by following the intentions and indications of the composer.

The struggle with the so-called "mentally lazy" is, of course, a difficult one. It is necessary to convince the pupil that the memorizing of single measures and short passages will train the memory and that such training will not involve unconquerable difficulties. In my book, "The Shortest Way to Pianistic Perfection," I have shown that mind training is accomplished through reflection. As a model example for reflection, I have analyzed an Etude, two Inventions of Bach and a Beethoven Sonata. Points of conjecture for reflection can be found very easily, but, naturally, there are also sections which are hard to memorize and where one encounters great difficulties.

The importance of reflection, which, in spite of its advantages, is appreciated very little and used seldom, causes me to analyze the French Suite in E major by Bach as a further example. The scanning of its "Note-picture" will easily and quickly serve as a means to its impressiveness. Contrary to this, it will seem as though the illustration of reflection which is used for enlightenment is often far-fetched and made up of so many words that one might think it useless and a waste of time.

I hope that my directions, which should immediately be transferred to the "Note-picture" of every single measure, will be understood instantly. My earnest advice is: Do not proceed from measure to measure until you have entirely memorized the *first measure;* thereafter selecting only a few measures at a time which must, of course, be practiced four to six times in the course of a day. In this manner, I have discovered, almost without exception, that my pupils have mastered and committed to memory all passages of the Allemande with absolute certainty in a comparatively few days. When teaching, I always demanded (in varied order) marked places (such as D, D-sharp passage, bass melody, sixth cadence) which the pupils would then play in proper tempo with proper fingering, etc., with little hesitation or delay. Although the marking of single measures isn't exactly necessary, it may be advantageous in accomplishing the task of memorization. Reflection, itself, must be comprehended gradually and independently by the pupil. A competent teacher should be able to direct him on this point. The capability of memorizing in this manner will grow extraordinarily and rapidly. Many pupils, after one year of this practice, have been able to memorize several pages from lesson to lesson. In many cases, my pupils have furnished proof that with the training of the memory one can obtain excellent results, and that it will pay to undertake all studies in the proposed manner.

Allemande of the French Suite in E Major by Bach

Key—E major. Time 4/4. Count loudly and shortly. The first measure for the right hand consists of chord tones of the E major triad with two passing notes in the following manner: After the up-beat B, the E major triad follows, starting with g-sharp, a as passing note; chord tone b, chord tones e″ e′ e″, f-sharp as passing note, e″. Then follows the exact repetition of the first half of the measure. The left hand begins on the second eighth note and consists of the E major tones in eighth notes: e, g-sharp, b, e′ and repetition of the E major triad. The second measure for left hand begins with e′ and for right hand with g-sharp′. When studying these measures, we commonly close with the first tone of the ensuing measure in order to impress "position and fingering" with absolute certainty. We shall call the second measure the "tri-tone-measure" since it contains the tones e″ f-sharp″ g-sharp″, being repeated after the lower seventh a. Thus is the following course: Right hand—g-sharp′ e″ f-sharp″ g-sharp″ a′ g-sharp″ f-sharp″ e″, then comes d-sharp″ as the "third" of the now following dominant triad b d-sharp f-sharp with the passing note e″ and finally the diminished "third" d″. The left hand has the four scale formed tones e′ d-sharp′ c-sharp′ and then, with the omission of b, the small a, the second half again has the analogical scale tones from b on, b a g-sharp e. This measure, too, is easy to remember. The third measure begins with the tones c-sharp″ right and left. We'll name it sixth cadence. After c-sharp″, as the "third" of the sub-dominant, the passing note d-sharp″ follows; then e″ a″ a′ aa″ c-sharp″ a″. The frame work is the sixths c-sharp″ a″: b′ g-sharp″; a′ f-sharp″; in the fourth measure g-sharp′ e″; f-sharp′ d-sharp″. The sixths partly follow immediately on the first tone or are delayed until the end of the quarter note. The first sixth proceeds in direct succession. The second sixth b′ g-sharp″ is delayed through the seventh a″ and

84

fundamental tone e″. The third sixth a′ f-sharp″ is delayed through b′ c-sharp″. The fourth sixth is direct. The fifth one is again delayed through g-sharp′ a′. Thereupon, the fundamental tone e″ follows. The "left" descends from small a to d-sharp in scale form. Now the sub-dominant triad (e c-sharp a) follows; then four tones b g-sharp a b; the tonic-triad, E major. The next two measures (5 and 6) we will call the "Chord-spot." The left hand part consists only of perfect chords, whereas, in the right hand part, the chord progressions are interrupted by intermediate tones. At this place, we begin with the up-beat g-sharp″ d-sharp″ f-sharp″. The first tones in measure "five" are e″ (right hand); left hand, small c-sharp. Then we must bear in mind the chord tones at the beginning of both measures: c-sharp e g-sharp, and one tone lower, b d-sharp f-sharp. In the second half of measures five and six, these chord tones, f-sharp a-sharp, c-sharp and e g-sharp b, follow a fifth lower each time. The right hand begins with e″ c-sharp″, between them the passing tone d-sharp″, then e″ g-sharp″ c-sharp″ e″ and b′ as transition to the next chord. The second chord a-sharp′ f-sharp′ with intermediate tone g-sharp′, a-sharp′ c-sharp″ f-sharp′, seventh e″ and f-sharp′. The third chord is the exact sequence of the preceding from d-sharp″ on. In the "left," the chords are the same. The chord tones follow one another alternately in contrary motion. Measures 7 and 8, we shall call the scale cadence. The left hand begins with the small e; after that, from c-sharp on, the B-major scale to b with intermediate tone f-sharp before b. Then cadence tones e f-sharp F-sharp B. The right hand has the scale tones from c-sharp″ to g-sharp″ up and down, only f-sharp missing when scale ascends. After that, the B-major scale from b″ to c-sharp″ with intermediate tone e″. Then mordent on d-sharp″, mordent on c-sharp″, closing tone b′. Measure 9, with preceding up-beat, is called six-five-four position. The right hand tones consist of dominant tones b d-sharp f-sharp; after that, first chord tone f-sharp″ with sixth a-sharp′; second chord tone d-sharp″ with fifth g-sharp′; third chord tone b′ with fourth f-sharp′. The left hand has B major triad with passing c-sharp; after that, b f-sharp b e, then the opening theme of the first measure from d-sharp on which passes through to measure 11 as sequence. The sixth sequence in the right hand follows, same beginning in the ninth measure with sixth g-sharp′ e″, then a-sharp′ f-sharp″, b′ g-sharp″, then triad b″ g-sharp″ e″, the scale tones g-sharp″ to b′; thereafter, chord tones g-sharp″ b′, mordent on a-sharp″, then, as an ending, triad B major with intermediate c-sharp″. In the left hand, cadence tones b g-sharp e f-sharp follow and also the B-major triad. The thirteenth measure has exactly the same setting as the first, only in B major instead of E major (also B major with the intermediate e″ and c-sharp″). Measure 14 begins (right hand) with d-sharp″ and b with left hand, and is, for the rest, similar to the second measure. We therefore call it the tri-tone measure of the second page. Although the three tones come after the "sixth" in the second measure, here they occur after the "third." The return of the three tones ensues again after the "seventh"; then E major in reverse progression, as in measure 2—B major. The left hand has the descending

French Suite VI

J. S. BACH

Allemande

B major triad with ensuing sub-dominant tone. The fourth quarter beat (left hand) is already the up-beat of measures 15 and 16, which we call bass melody. It is easy to commit this bass melody to memory with the scale formed tones e' d-sharp' c-sharp' b-sharp' (with omission of a-sharp), then g-sharp and the closing tones— small c-sharp C-sharp. This scale group repeats itself in measure 16 from c-sharp' on; and namely the tones c-sharp' b a g-sharp, with the omission of f-sharp to e, then closing tone a. The right hand part of measures 15 and 16 consists of chord tones of the "dominant seventh" chord of c-sharp minor. The tones are a-sharp' b-sharp' c-sharp" f-sharp" d-sharp" f-sharp" b-sharp' f-sharp", then resolving into c-sharp minor. The sixteenth measure is a sequence measure, a third lower. Measure 17 opens with d" (right hand), with f-sharp (left hand). We shall call measures 17 and 18 the "D, D-sharp spot." The right hand contains D major, with only one intermediate tone e. The eighteenth measure is exactly alike, only here, we have d-sharp" instead of d", and b-sharp' instead of a'. The third quarter beat begins with f-sharp each time. The left hand already begins with a g on the up-beat in measure 16, then follows the small motif (a g f-sharp), which repeats itself. Measures 19 and 20, we shall call the "seventh" cadence. Here we have (right hand) the "sevenths" g-sharp" e" c-sharp" a'; then f-sharp" d-sharp" b-sharp' g-sharp'; thereupon, the tones of the final cadence: e" d-sharp" c-sharp" e", g-sharp' c-sharp" d-sharp" b-sharp', c-sharp". In the left hand, the easily remembered three motif tones of the preceding measures are led through sequentially to the last cadence tones c-sharp f-sharp g-sharp G-sharp. We will call measures 20 to 22 the "parallel location" to the six-five-four position which is worked out as "sixth" position here. First of all, it is based upon c-sharp minor. The c-sharp minor chord tones c-sharp" g-sharp" e" c-sharp" e" come in the right hand; whereupon, the skip of a "sixth" down to g-sharp' occurs, which resolves into a'. Then come the chord tones c-sharp" a' f-sharp', a', and now again follows the "sixth" c-sharp, resolving into d-sharp. Then the entire group is repeated one tone lower. In the left hand, we have the chord tones c-sharp e g-sharp c-sharp', with the passing note g-sharp. The motif of right and left hands repeats a tone lower. Now (in measures 22, 23, 24) comes the parallel place to the "sixth" position with the ensuing cadence. It begins with c-sharp' a' f-sharp' in the right hand, followed by the second "sixth" d-sharp' b' g-sharp', then the third "sixth" e' c-sharp", then, after d-sharp", the chord tones e" c-sharp" a', the scale tones from c-sharp" down to e', repetition of tones c-sharp" e' with the intermediate shake (trill) on f-sharp'. The left hand corresponds exactly with the former "parallel place." Measures 26 and 27 give us the parallel chord location, the chords e g-sharp b, a c-sharp e, f-sharp a-sharp c-sharp, b d-sharp f-sharp. The right hand, as in the first chord place, opens the measure; but, contrary to that measure, here it moves upward, whereas, there it moves downward. The final tones in the right hand bring a deviation, which we must bear in mind. The final cadence of measures 27 and 28 contains the tones d-sharp" to a" and back again, and then

also the E major scale from b″ to b′—the cadence tones, "fourth"—
e″ b′, the "third"—c-sharp″ a′, then two "sixths" g-sharp′ e″,
f-sharp′ d-sharp″, and closing tone e″. The left hand has the dominant triad along with both fundamental tones of the "sub-dominant,"
once again the dominant and then the tonic.

II. TECHNIQUE THROUGH MENTAL WORK

Generally, no clear opinions exist as to the usefulness of mental work in order to acquire a good technique. We do not seem to know exactly what it means or how to develop technique through "brain work."

Technique, when playing an instrument, means controlling the fingers. Generally, it is used only in a limited sense regarding fluency, rapid execution of difficult passages and steady aim.

In order to acquire a perfect technique through brain work, an exact impression of the note picture upon the mind is the first problem which we must solve. Thereafter we should busy ourselves with the study in question, as to fingering, touch, note value, etc., to achieve perfection along these lines in the broadest sense. This occurs quickest and completely through intensive concentration of all intellectual powers and is, therefore, strenuous brain work. Contrary to this, others (namely the greater majority of music students) try to acquire technique by simply playing difficult sections as many times as possible with very little or no concentration. They gradually master these technical problems subconsciously, or, as the saying goes, "They have it in the fingers." A small minority boasts of this natural propensity. It sometimes takes many months to master difficult parts. Very many aspirants, who follow this mode of practice, never see the desired results in a lifetime. Such skill is unreliable. One's memory often goes "blank," and the cleanness of technique is seldom fully attained. A feeling of unsteadiness prevails, which tends to excite the nerves, especially when one appears before an audience. Stage fright is the outcome of it all, which seldom leaves such an afflicted performer. Many know only the above-mentioned way of practice, because it is more convenient than the intensive mental way of studying, and therefore preferred. In reality, it requires more time, never leading to perfection.

I shall now mention several exercises for the development of fingers and shall also touch upon finger control, which must be accomplished through continuous concentration. As the first technical exercise, we shall use the note material of the first two-part Invention by Bach.

I usually have the motif of this Invention played slowly enough for the metronomical setting, $\eighth = 70$. The brain matter must now function as a control for the most correct finger execution. First, it is limited to the practicing of the tones to a dynamic degree between *piano* and *pianissimo*, continuing the practice until the tones sound dynamically equal and at exact intervals. This exercise will train the ear to such an extent that in a few days the pupils will hear more distinctly and better. They learn to discriminate between loud and soft tones. They conceive the exact lengths of tone and feel their values. It is hardly deemed necessary by many to study in this technical manner, yet it has an essential effect upon the ear. Only those who receive this detached explanation will understand it, since they may not be accustomed to observe the slight variations which invariably occur. One does not emphasize such fluctuations sufficiently, even though they influence the characteristic parts.

As a further continuation of this subject, the following is important: Gradually speed up the tempo of the first exercise until the proper measure of time is attained. One should then select very short, fragmentary and difficult passages of a composition which are to be studied and reviewed. The student should begin very slowly, as in the first exercise, accelerating the tempo little by little, but not too quickly, until the exercise can be played faultlessly. In this manner, portion after portion should be connected until the single phrases are complete. Attempting more extended phrases is not advisable, as it leads to superficialities. Grouping the completed phrases later on will enable us to understand the construction of a composition and to render its contents fittingly.

It has always seemed peculiar to me that so little attention is paid to tone lengths, as, for instance, is necessary for the absolute and exact rendition in the *Cantilena* style. The inner warmth and feeling can be increased, the delivery becomes more ardent, if the absolute tone lengths are observed. Many excuses are given for uneven time. Often the extensive lineal structure is blamed for these shortcomings. In my opinion, it is this lineal structure which is dependent upon the painful working out of small motives and phrases. Even eminent virtuosi and noted conductors often "crowd in" endings of motives and phrases, seemingly unaware of it, or else attributing it to temperament and thereby entering upon the new idea or phrase ahead of time. The calmness in expression is lost, leaving a hasty and hurried impression. As the performer continues, the successive ideas become bunched together, because they are devoid of the lineal structure. Many players might object to climaxes wherein a *stretto* or an *accelerando* is used, claiming that "raising their effect" would be out of the question. This, however, is not the case.

Symmetrical intensification must also be warranted within an *accelerando* or a sensible *rubato*. If there is an exception to this rule, it is because of the nature of a composition.

An understanding of the exact duration of notes and the designated forces of tones (dynamics) must be taught. The teacher should continually draw his pupils' attention to errors which result from unevenness. It is with the study of dynamics that the real value of finger development comes into its own. In endeavoring to apply the same strength with every finger, you will notice that the thumb, due to its natural position, invariably strikes too softly, the second and third too loudly, the fourth weakest of all, and the fifth, owing to its shortness, necessitates greater energy.* Attaining an

---

* Additional reference: General hints on the practicability of all kinds of touch. Page 110.

even touch with all five fingers is a difficult task and depends essentially upon proper ear training. If these exercises are carried out six or eight times daily, under the guidance of the teacher (whom you visit at least three times a week) rapid progress will be the reward. Patience and concentration are the most important things. The student should constantly strive to improve the finger touch, relaxing the muscles not engaged. He should aim to better the carrying out of a *pianissimo* and slow succession of tones (in tempo, about 70 M.M.). These are problems which the pupil must solve and which will be of great aid in the development of the *legatissimo* touch. One must hold down each key and, at the same time, find out or feel what strength is necessary for every finger in order to bring out the required tonal effect. This is essential for the acquirement of technique. Pupils will be surprised to learn that through relaxation, they will gradually be able to play evenly, in a faster tempo, with an ease unknown to them a short while before. They are astounded, because they believe that they have accomplished this without the aid of technical studies, with which they dealt when they formerly practiced finger exercises and scales. Of course, all methods of touch and movements which we used were also technical exercises, but due to the said concentration, they showed their effectiveness more quickly. In my opinion, studies and finger exercises are superfluous, excepting in a small measure, for beginners. As we already have stressed, it is best to select the necessary mechanical problems from each new work which we intend to study.

III. RHYTHMICS

It is a known fact that strictly rhythmical playing is exceedingly effective. Rhythmical feeling is developed easily, provided that the music students have talent in sufficient measure along these lines. Teachers should already begin to develop it in children.

I shall now point out the ways and means of finger execution in the following lines. The carrying out of a strict rhythm is vitally important, because the character of a composition often hinges upon it. I shall show the importance of strict counting of uniform measurements and the playing of notes of equal value. If the pupil has arrived at the point where he hears and carries out exactly the smallest measurements of time, he has progressed in ear training to such an extent in the course of days that he hears and feels more keenly than those who have studied for years. Those others, who possibly have a good ear but are unable to hear the minute differences (because they were never shown and never knew their importance), will, therefore, never learn them. It may seem peculiar to my readers when I say that not one pianist who came to me for a broader musical education showed signs of such time discrimination, which gave proof that ear training had been sadly neglected. Even pianists who had often appeared in concerts proved to me in private that they were unable to count while practicing, and when they did count, it was irregular, utterly worthless and useless. With endless pains, I finally succeeded in enabling them to count rhythmically. Only then, when the pupil is capable of carrying out single parts metronomically, will I show him the free style of playing, whereas I frequently allow liberties in rhythm and tempo, I have always found that, in adhering to a metronomical pace, many rhythmical liberties eventually develop without any effort of feeling. On the other hand, there exists playing, based upon incorrect counting, which cannot be corrected later nor be impressed upon the ear. These are experimental facts. I shall also aver that ninety per cent of all mistakes are rhythmical mistakes caused by carelessness in the holding out of notes and the observance of pauses (rests) in accordance with their value. Many players imagine they have reached a point of perfect rhythm through the use of the metronome. They do not seem to hear, however, the minute differences when a tutor tries to convince them that in the course of lengthy sections and parts they have failed to synchronize with the metronome; in fact, they cannot understand that they played *out of time* in many instances. I do not deem it pedantic to combat such minute irregularities, since they often disturb the calm and serenity which are essential to a melodic rendition. Whereas painting, sculpturing and architecture exist as transient cultural (or static) arts, the art of dancing, music, poetry and oratory—the dynamic arts—in their phases, are subjected to lapse of time.

Measurement or division, with respect to time in the reproduction of musical compositions, is taught under the heading of rhythmics.

Metre is the designation for the duration of "counts" and whatever embraces them. It is also customary to use the word rhythm instead, which in a smaller measure pertains exclusively to the comparative lengths of tones and their accentuation. Tutors who know the correct definition of *both words* often accept this term.

Rhythmics (from the Greek) is the study of rhythm in a language or in music. Rhythmic (according to the dictionary) means measured motion, marked by regular recurrence, as of quantity, accent, etc.*

We might well assume that rhythm first prevailed in the dance and from there passed over to "word" and "tone," from whence the poetical and musical art emanated.

Rhythm is next in importance to melody and form.

As a melody is comprised of a number of variously pitched tones, so does rhythm measure the motion of successive tones, with respect to unity of time (in physics units of time refer to seconds) which we can easily understand and feel. No matter how many "time units" we compile (say one, two, three, four, six, etc.), we end this unity through a vertical line on the staff and call it a "measure" in notation.

In order to establish the proper duration of note values, the composer signifies a certain time and therein creates the measures, which continue throughout the full length of a composition. This accurate (divisional) arrangement is comparatively new. In fact, such time divisions did not exist in the sixteenth century. They were, moreover, developed gradually. First of all, let us presume that single sections of a composition can be written in different kinds of time. The measure itself will consist of several equal counts, which, in other words, are equal fractions of a measure. In the note system, they are also called breaks. Generally, a whole measure is divided into two- or three-part counts (maybe four counts), it all depending upon whether the unit or picture notes (1/4, 1/8, 1/2) are used. The time signature is simply written at the beginning of a piece, either 4/4, 4/8, 4/2, etc., or 3/8, 3/4, 3/2, etc. The unit counts can consist of whole, half, quarter, eighths, sixteenths, etc., so that all kinds of fractions will be possible in the measures themselves or in the various note denominations thereof. Usually we do not employ fractions beyond the "sixty-fourths," since they are less comprehensive. Seldom do we use those that are grouped in numbers of five, seven, etc.

The order of time is determined by the number of parts in a measure plain or subdivided. The plain order has two or three parts; the "subdivided" has fractional equivalents. As has been

---

* Originally the word rhythm meant "flowing motion." In our present music, this motion is based on periodical divisions, called measures.

94

said, the time within a piece can be changed. We simply change the time signature when entering into a new phase of the composition.

The arranging of notes within a measure is done arithmetically. If, for instance, we had common time, where we count by quarters, and play four notes on each quarter beat, these notes would be written as sixteenths. In common time we classify and write notes as follows: Whole note, $\circ$; half note, $\lozenge$; quarter note, $\lozenge$; eighth note, $\lozenge$; sixteenth note, $\lozenge$; etc. A dot after a note prolongs the note one-half of its value, so that a $\circ\cdot$ would contain 3/2, a $\lozenge$. 3/4, a $\lozenge$., 3/8, etc. A second dot again prolongs the value of the first dot one-half of its value, as follows: $\circ\cdot\cdot = 7/4$; $\lozenge.. = 7/8$; $\lozenge..$ = 7/16, etc.

For the rests we have the following characters: $\blacktriangledown$ = whole rest; $\blacksquare$ = half rest; ξ = quarter rest; γ = eighth rest; $\mathcal{7}$ = sixteenth rest, etc. These can also be prolonged through dots. It seems peculiar and unbelievable that many advanced players are often unacquainted with these characters, and yet it is a fact.

Pedagogical Hints

The procedure of dividing (cutting up) measures and summing up their fractional values is an essential and very important task for pupils. This cutting up of measures should be practiced until one has completely mastered all kinds of divisions. Teachers should give their pupils difficult examples progressively, such as will be found in the slow movements of Sonatas, by Haydn. Sometimes we come across pupils who play certain passages of very difficult works by ear, who worry little or none about keeping strict time. It is the teacher's main duty to teach his pupils the value of musical independency, which requires an educational capacity for the understanding of metrical calculation in music.

Take for example: Second Movement of Concerto for Piano in C-minor by L. van Beethoven, Op. 37.

Second Movement of Concerto for two Pianos and Pedal in C-major, by J. S. Bach.

Musical rhythm (according to Dr. Reisman in his "Esthetics") has a dual sense: (1) Extensive rhythm, which pertains to the pro-

95

longation of sounds, and (2) Intensive rhythm, which pertains to the inflection (rising and falling) of tone; in other words, the accentuated and unaccentuated members of a measure. Accentuation of certain beats gives evidence of rhythm. In order to announce each new measure, we accent the first beat of the same. The regular recurrence of accentuated and unaccentuated beats is the primary step to rhythmic construction. The accentuated beats are the strong (Thesis-fall), the unaccentuated beats are the weak (Arsis-rise). This natural accent of each measure, which we term the metrical accent, differs somewhat from the rhythmical accents which we shall explain later.

The full metrical accent always falls on the first or principal beat of a measure. In the common time of 4/4 we also have a secondary accent which falls on the third beat; in 6/8 time this accent falls on the fourth beat. In 9/8 time we have the main accent 1, the secondary accents 4 and 7. In 12/8 time we have the main accent 1, the secondary accents 4, 7 and 10.

It is possible to cut up the above accents into still smaller relative members, in so far as the denominational groups and equivalents are concerned. Of course, there is a limit; otherwise this rhythmical matter would become too complicated, making it almost impossible for one to understand it. There is one example which needs attention, namely, the difference in treating eighth notes when they occur in 3/4 and 6/8 time. In the first illustration: 3/4 time— ♪ ♪ ♪ ♪ ♪ ♪ the main accent falls on the first eighth note, secondary accents on third and fifth eighth notes. In the second illustration: 6/8 time, ♪ ♪ ♪ ♪ ♪ ♪ the main accent falls on the first eighth note, the secondary accent on the fourth eighth note.

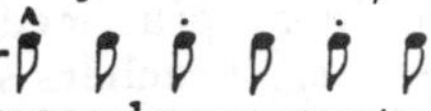

Triplets, quintuplets, as well as sextuplets, etc., have only one accent (on their first note), which must recur uninterruptedly and quickly, so as to become a direct and accurate division of a measure.

Couplets, Quadruplets, etc.

Whenever we separate (or cut up) "three-part" valued notes, we substitute dots to signify their ratings, as, for instance, in the following illustration:

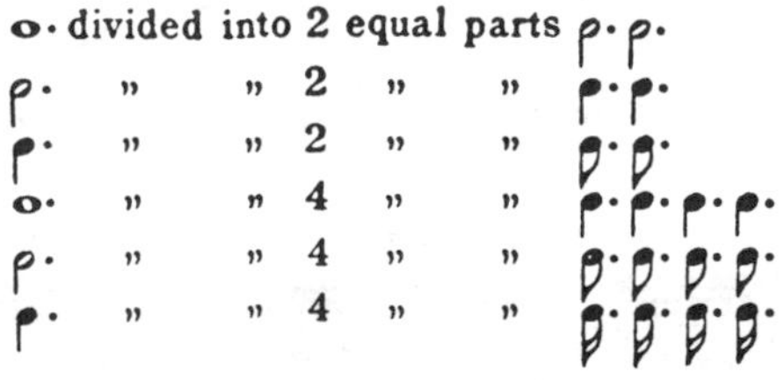

o· divided into 2 equal parts ♩· ♩·

♩· ” ” 2 ” ” ♩·♩·

♩· ” ” 2 ” ” ♩·♩·

o· ” ” 4 ” ” ♩·♩·♩·♩·

♩· ” ” 4 ” ” ♩·♩·♩·♩·

♩· ” ” 4 ” ” ♩·♩·♩·♩·

To facilitate the reading of all such separations, we use the nearest *full valued* notes instead of the dotted ones, writing a slur over them and indicating the number of notes therein by a numeral.

96

In this manner, we also formulate without exception all denomina- tions of notes, thereby giving the reader a clearer conception of notation, plain and subdivided. All groupings, such as couplets, triplets, quadruplets, etc., can then be easily determined.

Illustration:

The Up-beat

Any portion (or part) of a piece which does not start with a full-time measure, but which takes an intrinsic part in the motif belonging to the down-beat, is, in its entirety, called the "up-beat." The up-beat of a motif is (according to Riemann), not only a possible form, but the actual source or original form of musical life. In general, the closing measure of a piece that begins with an up-beat is looked upon as a supplement of the note values to the up-beat.

The Syncope

The syncope is a rhythmically interesting feature. A syncope is the designation of a tone which enters upon a weak beat, being sustained throughout the strong beat. In other words, it is the negative of the metrical accent.

When we hear an unusually long stretch of consecutive syncopes, we lose the feeling for natural time beats, unless the same is accompanied by a metrical figure. Syncopation is felt just as long as metrical accentuation subsists. When we refer to harmony, the syncope is to be conceived as either a prolonged tone of a chord into an ensuing chord or as an anticipation note. The application of the syncope can be traced back to the pre-Bach period. Mozart used it abundantly; Beethoven also made use of it repeatedly with particular effect. Both Schumann and Brahms used it excessively, so that it hardly has the syncopated effect in some places, as, for instance, in the first sub-theme of Schumann's "Carnival Jests" (Faschingsschwank) (First Movement) in E flat.

The metrical accent does not always coexist with the rhythmical accent. When delivering a piece, it is most essential to observe the rhythmical accents. We have frequently seen (in the case of the syncope) how the metrical accent is taken up by the rhythmical accent. As a further illustration, let me draw your attention to the Mazurka (3/4 time) in which the second quarter, known as the weak beat, receives a special accent.

The sustaining of uniform time units is not easy, because it necessitates a rhythmical inclination which can be promoted through practice. A pupil who is accustomed to playing unrhythmically can

97

hardly be cured of this habit later on. The unrhythmical rendition of a composition is intolerable and unbearable to every musical person, who would rather hear false notes than tolerate rhythmical errors.

Musicians should pay more attention to rhythm than to melodic progression, since the latter is easier to bear in mind, with less need for precise control.

The rhythmical inclination of pupils varies decidedly. What should be done to enable less rhythmically talented pupils to keep strict time? Many methods have been tried. The French Swiss Jaques Dalcroze, for instance, tries to accomplish it through rhythmical gymnastics. Many of his pupils have undoubtedly shown surprising results, principally because of the above training.

In my opinion, very short and loud counting is the best remedy for the successful training of rhythmical feeling. Of course, this is impossible for singers and players of wind instruments, although they must also acquire this keen rhythmical feeling through previous counting in one way or another. The clapping of hands and stamping of feet are uncertain methods, having insufficient significance in the delicate training of the ear. A poorly trained ear is a barrier in the realm of music. I know that my opinions are opposed by modern colleges, which do not even permit counting while playing. When an artist such as Gieseking admits that he still counts occasionally, and Professor Straube, when instructing his choristers, marks the rhythm by counting keenly and even tapping certain singers on the shoulders, I am convinced that this is the proper way of developing rhythmical feeling. Both artists support my ideas.

How can one profit by counting?

1. *Exercise:* The pupil should set the metronome at 60, uttering the numeral "one" (1) shortly and snappily at every metronomical beat, in this way training the ear to listen carefully, in order to discover whether or not this outspoken numeral "one" synchronizes with the metronomical beat. At first, he will feel as if his oral count occurs earlier or later than the metronomical beat. He will also come to the conclusion that the task of properly sustaining notes is more difficult than he imagined and that it will take extensive training to keep up with the metronome.

2. *Exercise:* At each metronomical beat = 60, count two numerals (one-two) shortly and snappily until the respective units of time synchronize exactly.

3. *Exercise:* Set the metronome at 46 and count three time-units to every beat.

After mastering these three exercises, continue as follows:

4. *Exercise:* (The metronome is ticking uninterruptedly at 46.) Count two time-units five times in succession and then three time-units five times in succession. Do these alternately and without interruption. Then count (without interruption) two and three

98

time-units four times, three times, twice and finally two and three time-units in rapid succession.

The following exercise, playing two and three notes in succession in strict time, means properly matching plain eighth notes and alternating triplets consecutively as equivalents of quarter notes. Such figures occasionally occur in musical literature. These, however, are carried out properly by only a small number of musicians. Many are not aware of this deficiency because of the lack of ear training; others deem it too pedantic to adhere to accuracy. I should like to emphasize that such accuracy is very important with regard to many characteristics of a composition. It should now be clear to each player that he must also try these exercises without the aid of a metronome, because it is taken for granted that he has now developed an inner and independent rhythmical feeling which will not always necessitate loud counting.

When counting while playing, the student should observe the following: Be careful, when counting eighth notes, that no unevenness ensues. Count "one-and-two-and-three-," etc., real shortly, uttering no other syllables between these words, since the "drawing together" of such utterances will cause unequal spacing of time. Also count loudly when playing the most simple exercises. Unevenness often occurs when a passage is not mastered technically. In this case a pause ensues while counting. The fact is, the player must first find the proper tones on the instrument. If this happens, beginners have no other alternative than to study their small pieces by bits and according to their intervals, without observing the rhythm. The young performer should practice such small sections until his playing has reached the point of certainty. Pupils who are rhythmically trained in this manner from the very beginning give the teacher very little trouble in the future.

Rhythmical difficulties ensue in ensemble or part playing when two notes are played against three, as, for instance, in piano playing, where the right hand has two eighths on a quarter beat and the left hand has triplets against the same; or in the case of six notes being played on a quarter, where both notes of the right hand fall on 1 and 4 and those of the left hand on 1, 3 and 5. The entry of each tone, in the case of three against four notes, can also be figured out mathematically. Although the difficulty lies in the "playing together" of parts, one might do well to practice with each hand separately. Breithaupt is of the opinion that such preparatory exercises have little value. He further claims that a better ensemble can be produced through a good "approach" and "entry." But experience teaches us that these very preparatory exercises are an indispensable aid to the so-called "approach" and "entry" for both hands.

There is one error which should be censured whenever apparent, that of shortening the value of notes (also called stealing of time). An illustration of this common mistake is playing faster when greater valued notes follow the lesser ones, as in the case of "halves" and "quarters" following "sixteenths." The same bad habit exists regarding rests and pauses. Many players disregard the fact that

99

pauses and rests within the phrases, at the endings of phrases, as well as at the close of a part, are as important as the notes. Both notes and rests are component factors in the metrical and rhythmical sense. Although loud and exact counting is essential to keeping strict time, it is also advisable to refrain from continuous counting in the case of similar consecutive figures. As the pupil advances in this particular branch, he must become able to play rhythmically without oral counting. The metronome should be used temporarily as a time controller or as an emergency instrument, and not as a permanent medium.

Tempo

Tempo is dependent upon the measured units per second, which constitute the principal rhythmical pulses in a musical composition. The word "Tempo" in music, therefore, means the duration of time units in the space of time.

The composer indicates his chosen tempi with terms such as *Allegro* (quick and lively), *Adagio* (very slow), *Presto* (as quickly as possible). For example, the duration of a quarter note would be shorter in *Allegro* than in *Adagio* tempo.

The above-mentioned terms, however, do not alter the note values. We shall touch upon acceleration and retardation later on. If we choose the quarter note as the main pulse unit and play 120 quarters per minute, we shall notice that there are two quarters per second. In the eighteenth century Maelzel invented the mechanical instrument called the metronome (time meter), the purpose of which is the marking of strict time. This triangular shaped instrument consists of a clock work which sets a vertical pendulum into motion. This pendulum can be shortened by means of a sliding weight. When this is done, it swings to and fro more quickly. On the pendulum are found frets, which are numerated from 40 to 200. The sliding weight can be set at any given fret (or ridge) and will cause the pendulum to swing at the respective ratio per minute. For instance, if one pushes this weight to the number 100, the pendulum will swing 100 times per minute. One can hear a "click" with each swing. There can be no doubt as to the great importance of the metronome, since it is absolutely reliable as a time keeper. To make sure that a given tempo is strictly obeyed, the composer will indicate it metronomically. Although we have laid great stress upon strict time, it is sometimes necessary to take musical liberties, especially in places where no musical signs occur. To be a real artist, one must take such licenses. Individuality in playing is shown in this way. Riemann has coined the word "agogic," which he uses in expressing the many changes in tempo not indicated by the composer. The indicated changes in tempo, such as *rubato, accelerando, ritardando,* and also the dynamic entry, such as *diminuendo, crescendo,* etc., are used in a measure far beyond the non-designated "agogical" changes. One is naturally inclined to hurry when using a *crescendo* and to hold back (slow up) when using a *diminuendo.* In using an *accelerando,* one should not start too quickly as most players do. Remember, acceleration means, to hasten gradually until the climax is reached. The same error is reversed in the *ritardando*—here we start too slowly. This is often noticeable when concert pianists are accompanied by orchestras. Here the ensemble often suffers through the unmusical liberties which the pianist takes, precision being hampered by either "hanging over" or "running ahead," in spite of good leadership of the conductor. But if the pianist changes the tempi in such a manner that there is a mutual feeling between soloist and conductor, then the ensemble will function to perfection.

Of course, there are instances (for example, in *Cadenzas*) where a composer expects a freedom of delivery, leaving it to the discretion of the interpreter.

In order to increase the effect in declamatory music, it is sometimes necessary to pause before stressing certain tones, even though the composer has made no note of this in his score. This style of expression has a tendency to keep the listener in a momentary suspense and seems to excite his interest to a high degree. The application of the agogic hold becomes more impressive in a melody, even when it is played *pianissimo*. This idea of artistic expression should not be underestimated. Of course, there is a limit to this method of playing. Abuse of it will disturb the melodic flow and give the whole performance an air of affectation. Many pianists use this "agogic" pause excessively in the *Cantilenas* as documentary evidence of their feeling, of course, in a disturbing manner. This pause is also used before entering upon new phrases, new parts or final settings. Sometimes it occurs as a sudden break or as a surprise to the audience, causing them to anticipate something more outstanding. Hans von Bülow made clever and successful use of this latter pause in Beethoven Symphonies and others, widely advocating the same.

The motion of a piece is sometimes interrupted (after a *ritardando*) by a hold, while a tone, a chord or a pause is prolonged beyond its value. This hold is indicated by a sign ⌒ called the "*Fermate*" whose duration (time value) is left to the discretion of the player.

There are no fixed rules for the prolongation of a *Fermate*. It depends upon the tempi and is principally prolonged at endings. At times the general yielding of voice and instrument also play a part in its length. Anyone possessing rhythmical feeling can easily match the value of a *Fermate* with the phrase in which it occurs in accordance with the fixed tempo in which the whole composition is played or sung. Bülow recognized the musical talent of a pianist by the way he prolonged the *Fermate*. Sometimes the *Fermate* is written above the bar line, which separates two measures. When *Fermates* occur over the notes of middle sections, their duration is shorter than when they are written over the final note of a piece.

Fermates usually lead into the *Cadenzas* of *Concertos*. Here the free style, the "*tempo rubato*," comes into its own. The *Cadenza* is an ornamental bridge between two parts. Almost every large *Concerto* contains one or more *Cadenzas*, which give the performer

101

an opportunity to demonstrate his virtuosity.   Formerly the soloists would either write their own *Cadenzas* or improvise them.

There is quite a difference between large and small *Cadenzas*. The small *Cadenza* consists of a number of tones, passages and figures which are not arranged in measures.   The large *Cadenza* is "measured" and worked out thematically.   In other words, it is based on such passages and figures as are found in the broader themes of the respective movement.   It is sometimes a very expansive part of the principal work and is easily recognized as a vital part of the whole work, as in the Piano *Concerto* by Schumann, where it becomes an inserted constituent part.   The small *Cadenza* is played in free tempo, which naturally must be relative to the tempo of the piece in question.

The note values of the *Cadenza* are not governed by the designated tempo but are defined through their relation to one another.

Examples of small *Cadenzas* are: *Cadenzas* of First Movements in Phantasy in D minor, Mozart; Piano *Concerto* in E flat major, Beethoven.

All previous remarks on Rhythm, as well as those following on Dynamics, Exercises, etc., will be of interest to string and wind instrumentalists and should require but small modifications for practical performance.

IV. DYNAMICS

The word "Dynamics" comes from the Greek δύναμις and means power. In music it is defined as the "science of power, applied to tones in different degrees." It is this power which manifests itself in the antithesis of strong and weak, of increased and decreased swelling of tones. It is the force which influences our senses, which helps us to express our feelings of happiness, nobleness and grandeur, our feelings of oppression, anguish and sadness in music. Without dynamics, music would be less affected, inexpressive, uninteresting, so to say, lifeless, whereas, if applied cleverly, it will lend expression and plasticity to a composition. It was this perception that impelled great men and women to magnify the contrasts of life, as time elapsed, in Orchestral Music (which in Haydn's Symphonies was a mere rustle compared with the storm in the musical works of Wagner, Berlioz, and R. Strauss), and in piano music. In the days of the clavichord, the piano makers were bent on tone perfection. Today we are able to produce great tone volumes on the so-called "Concert Grand." Thus do the piano compositions give proof of formerly unthought of outbursts of force (we remind you of Liszt), which self-evidently have since become natural developments in the musical sphere. This does not mean that the piano player is a mere noise maker. He tries his utmost to produce a *pianissimo* which is hardly audible. In short, he aims to contrast his tones in all possible shades.

As signs for the various degrees of force, we use to a large degree Italian words or abbreviations; less seldom and only of late we have been using German terms. The following are the customary terms:

ff	= *fortissimo,*	very loud
f	= *forte,*	loud
poco f	= *poco forte,*	moderately loud
mf	= *mezzo forte,*	medium loud
mp	= *mezzo piano,*	medium soft (somewhat softer than *mf*)
p	= *piano,*	soft
pp	= *pianissimo,*	very soft

Many composers use *ppp* (*piano-pianissimo*), as soft as possible; *fff* (*forte-fortissimo*), as loud as possible. Even such signatures as *pppp* and *ffff* can be found.

For the gradual increasing of tone, we use the term *cresc.* (*crescendo*), swelling; for diminishing of tone, *decresc.* (*decrescendo*); or *dim.* (*diminuendo*), diminishing, decreasing.

Accentuation, Well Marked, Stressing a Tone are signified as follows: *sf* = *sforzato* or *sforzando*, explosive; *marcato* or *fp* = *forte-piano*, loud, then soft; or *pf* = *piano-forte* = soft, then loud. For the marking of each individual tone, we use the term *rinforz.* = *rinforzando.* Sometimes we add the following expressions to the previous terms: *molto*, much; *meno*, less; *poco a poco*, little by little; *subito*, suddenly; and others.

One should comprehend clearly that *ff*, *f*, *p*, etc., are relative terms and that they depend upon the tonal strength of an instrument as well as on the physical strength and capability of the player. For the tempo (time count), we have a standard of time unit called the "second," which is reproduced exactly by the metronome. Since we have no mechanical standard for tone volume, we leave it entirely to the discretion of the individual. The mighty thunder, which, for instance, Rubinstein could produce on the piano, could scarcely be accomplished by a young girl, who would otherwise play the same composition in a praiseworthy manner.

It is this very difference in the carrying out of the various degrees of force which conveys different pictures to different players. These differences distinguish the individual delivery, which makes the same composition appear interesting and worth hearing, leaving a new impression upon the audience whenever played by a strange performer.

The interpretation of the artist is based essentially on his different conceptions of the dynamic degrees. When we consider that each *piano*, each *forte*, each *crescendo* and each *diminuendo*, even each accent sounds differently no matter how often played by the same pianist, we realize how greatly the delivery of a piece depends upon the disposition of an artist. It is to the advantage of a player that no standard measure of tone exists. In consequence of this fact, we recognize the ingenuity and creative power of an interpreter.

The term *piano* means soft; *forte* means loud. There is a great difference between soft and loud, which many fail to understand. This difference is very important, especially when a *subito* follows a *f* or *ff* or a *p* and *pp;* in other words, when a sudden change must take place. Beethoven took great pleasure in using these strong contrasts. Just as the consonant must be pronounced distinctly at the end of each word when we recite poetry, so must the musician work out the musical contrasts very distinctly. The player often thinks he is shading his tones, when the differences of his tones are mere blotches, due to faulty touch. One can either color too sparingly or too abundantly, thereby making a caricature of the musical picture.

It is much easier to play *fortissimo* than *pianissimo*. The deviations do not become too obvious to the ear. In the *pianissimo*, an unintentionally loud tone will strike the ear unpleasantly.

The *sforzando* should fit the character of the respective note and should in general be played less strongly in the moderately soft pieces than in the forceful *"bravura"* compositions. Here good taste is a very valuable factor. The sign > or ∧ signifies an accent, which indicates that the note is to be played softer than *sf*.

104

The rendition of an effective *crescendo* and *decrescendo* demands incessant practice. Here is what Bülow writes about them. *"Decrescendo* means *forte; crescendo* means *piano."* This popular rule, which should never have been formulated, will ever stand out in bold letters. An intolerable routine frequently exists, wherein the dynamical development is mistaken for a dynamical condition, namely, pounding when entering upon a *crescendo,* or rustling softly when starting a *diminuendo.* This is the proper way of playing a *crescendo:* Play the first tone in accordance with the previously indicated degree of force and then swell out gradually until you have reached its full height. The symbolical sign for a *crescendo* resembles a fork (or a hairpin) and illustrates graphically its occurrence, as you will see: ⎯⎯⎯⎯

The *decrescendo* points in the opposite direction: ══════
Writing or printing the signs in this manner ⎯⎐═══
═══════▷⎯ is wrong, because they do not illustrate their purpose properly.

Every known mode of touch is used in the execution of tone forces. The softest tones and chords are produced by laying the fingers on the keyboard, gently pressing down the keys. In order to produce loud tones, we apply a flexible swing of the fingers, the hand and the lower arm. Concerning the *fortissimo,* we thrust the entire arm toward the keys or in the vernacular, "play straight from the shoulder." For polyphonic pieces we use the pressure touch in a very particular measure. Many nuances are at our disposal from *pp* to *ff,* which we should employ to the fullest extent.

As a general rule, the melody should stand out against the accompaniment. In order to accomplish this, one hand must play stronger (louder) than the other. The melodic lead becomes more intricate when both the melodic tones and the accompanying figure are to be struck by the same hand. (Refer to Chopin's Etude, Op. 10, No. 3.) These by no means *slight technical* demands increase in polyphonic playing, wherein several voices (or parts), or at least their entries, must occasionally come into prominence. A lowering of the hand toward the key, which produces the melodic tone, will often be of great value to the touch.

Concerning the rendition of several consecutive chords, it is advisable, when aiming to produce a certain volume of tone, to bear in mind that the finger-tips should be in a level position and that both fingers and wrists must be firmly and not too weakly fixed if an equal pressure is to be applied to the ensuing touch. This mode of touch is a certain guarantee in so far as the quality of chord tones is concerned. It is also a safeguard against the bad habit of relying upon the pedal for the "holding of individual notes," where individual tones are often lost to the ear and omitted involuntarily.

By this time, you will most likely be convinced that dynamic shading is a great art which demands much practice, diligence and a constantly open ear. The pupil should be taught the importance of dynamics as soon as possible. The teacher should insist upon characteristic shading, no matter how unassuming the little compositions may be.

V. VARIETY OF TOUCH

In my first book, I purposely discussed definitely only the full-arm stroke and pressure touch. The remaining commonly used modes are treated by most teachers. On the other hand, the two mentioned above are either ignored or treated indifferently. In the ensuing chapter, I shall (because of many suggestions) present a summarized synopsis of the various kinds of touch, with which every pianist should become familiar.

In his book, "The Problem of Modern Pianoforte Technique," Eugene Tetzel deals with the physiological possibilities of touch in the following manner: He retains that which answers the purpose in the old school and omits that which goes beyond the limit in modern pedagogy. He defends opinions with which everybody should agree. He has expressed that which other pedagogues have applied practically, using the middle path which lies between the old and new systems. To these pedagogues, of course, Tetzel says little that is new. In spite of this, his viewpoint is applicable. We will not refute the fact that all necessary modes of touch were carried out instinctively by excellent pianists of the past. It is true, however, that not so long ago an investigation was made for the benefit of those who did not possess the inherent talent to apply the proper modes of touch instinctively. We learn through this retrospection that the old pedagogues (with few exceptions) taught their pupils many mistakes. They were good players but poor instructors. Not so very long ago it was customary and advisable to play each chord and each octave exclusively from the wrist. But the teachers themselves would not live up to this method. The last decades have undoubtedly repaid our survey along these lines. Pedagogy has advanced to great advantage in this branch of piano playing, the methodical touch. The suggestions of Deppe, Caland, Klose, Soechting, Dr. Steinhausen, Breithaupt and others have caused the stone of progress to roll, notwithstanding the fact that it has rolled too far in some respects, as, for instance, when Breithaupt dispensed almost entirely with finger development. This is an erroneous method which will lead to the eventual cramping of fingers and cause an irresistible weakening of their entire members. Remember, technique without finger development is unthinkable. Tetzel's views on "touch" are almost the same as those expressed throughout this book. The author based his instructions on these principles at least thirty years prior to the appearance of Tetzel's book.

Tetzel denotes the following possibilities for touch:

1. The free fall.
2. The throw, stroke, swing.
3. The roll.
4. The pressure.

In the fall, throw, stroke, swing, and partly the roll, the fingers hang suspended above the keys, whereas in the case of the pressure touch, the fingers rest upon the keys prior to the actual touch.

The Free Fall

The free fall in music is not identical with the free fall of a body in the physical sense. It resembles only the motion. Most likely that is why Deppe introduced the musical free fall. It can be extended to the whole arm, the lower arm, the wrist, or the fingers. The free fall in piano playing is effected in the following manner:

Bend the arm, keeping the elbow, wrist and fingers in a fixed position but free from stiffness. The fingers must be firmly set in order to strike the desired keys. The arm should fall loosely from the shoulder joint; the fingers should perform the function of aiming at the respective keys without unnecessary maneuvers.

As a preparatory exercise, I suggest the following: The pupil is reminded of the idle arm muscles while walking and is told to swing his arms like a pendulum. He is then taught to keep these muscles relaxed while raising the arm, thereupon dropping the latter through its own weight, like a dead object.

The free fall from the elbow demands a gentle fixation of the wrist and fingers, the latter being prepared to strike the respective keys. The upper arm should hang loosely in its socket; the combined fall and touch should occur in the same manner as the fall of the entire arm.

The free fall of the wrist calls for a fixation of the fingers, the upper arm hanging loosely, the lower arm fixed, in so far as the horizontal position demands it.

In the case of the free fall of the fingers, the finger members demand as much fixation as is necessary for the touch. The player dare not forget to keep his fingers in a curved position. Naturally, the greatest strength is attained through the fall of the whole arm. The free fall of the lower arm makes it possible to produce a strong *forte*, whereas the free fall of the wrist produces less tone volume and that of the fingers not more than a *pianissimo*, since the fingers are of slight weight and have only a one-inch fall. It takes quite a strong fixation for the development of *fortissimo* tones and chords. Many players call it rigidity.

The free fall and touch, which involve fixation, muscular action, firm strokes, flexible and relaxed arms, hands and fingers, can come into their own under one condition only, that is, if fatigue is never prevalent. Where fatigue begins, technique ends.

The free fall that has no additional features is only a theoretical mode of touch and cannot be applied practically.

The Throw and Stroke

The touch which concerns the throw consists of fixed fingers thrust from the knuckle joints or from the wrist by fixation of the knuckle joints. By a further fixation of the wrist and the additional

107

fixation of the elbow, both the lower and upper arms are automatically thrust along with them. The throw is accomplished through muscular strength, which transfers the weight of the hand to the lower and upper arm alternately, a throwing motion ensuing and the fixed fingers striking down the keys.

The word "stroke" is understood in the same sense as the word "touch." The player generally imagines that he must carry out these elements somewhat stronger and more expressively than ordinarily until his playing reaches the point of resistance. The distinction between the two modes becomes more difficult because of the similarity of both. For that reason it will not pay the pianist to make further inquiries as to their theoretical purpose. The combined mode of touch and throw, plus stroke, has become very popular among pianists, because it permits every imaginable nuance from *ff* to *pp* and is also a means of warding off fatigue. The throw and stroke are the usual modes of touch which result from the so-called "free fall." Their proper application is dependent upon such flexible muscles as are not immediately employed. This is best accomplished by letting the shoulder hang slightly but naturally. This position also permits the cooperation of the shoulder muscles, which otherwise would cause the muscles of the upper and lower arm to stiffen, thereby hindering their development. Càland calls this combined throw and free fall the "favorite free fall," speaking of it in contrary terms with regard to the "controlled fall," which is caused by the restraining of the swinging mass. These modes of the free fall are used extensively.

The Swing

The swing is a movement, a basic form of a pendulum sway, being elastic and reactive to the throw and stroke. It therefore modifies the latter and originates round, wavy movements.

The Roll

It is an established fact that roll movements can emanate from the shoulder or radius joint only. If the movements start from the shoulder, the elbow joint must become fixed; if they start from the radius joint, the upper arm must hang flexibly. In order to make this movement practical in piano playing, it will be necessary to fix the wrist, knuckle joint and fingers.

If we strike a tone (key) by means of pronation (for instance with the thumb), and let the higher octave follow with the fixed fifth finger through supination, we have what is called a roll, which, when carried out in uninterrupted, rapid succession, is termed a *tremolo*.

When either the thumb or the little finger holds down a note while other notes are being played, we have a "plain lateral stroke." In the first instance the thumb is the axis, and in the second, the little finger.

When the originally suppressed fingers are released with the strokes of the other fingers and a roll is carried out in the opposite direction, as in the *tremolo*, we call this dual movement the "mixed lateral stroke." In the octave *tremolo* the axis would therefore lie in the so-called center of gravity, as applied to length or space. For very loud playing we suggest the use of the upper arm roll. We can undertake rolls which begin *pianissimo* and which (through increasing centrifugal power) can be worked up to a *fortissimo*, thus permitting every possible nuance (refer to first book). The application of the roll movement shows its great usefulness by means of the exclusive use of the stronger lower arm and relative shoulder muscles, by which relative fatigue takes place more slowly. The elbow is raised when the roll movement is used. This is an absolutely natural movement and should be encouraged. There was a time when one was taught to clamp the elbow joint close to the body, in order to attain a quiet arm position. Such a suppression with regard to the lifting of the elbow joint is impossible. The attempt alone hinders the freedom of movement considerably. When exceptionally rapid tone progressions occur, one might dispense with the roll and use the plain finger touch. On the other hand, the roll is applied largely as a support to the fingers and also as an aid in warding off fatigue.

If the tension of the two fingers that appear as a lateral extreme point of a lever is great, a slight rolling movement is sufficient; if there is less tension, the touch demands a stronger rotation. The trill gives evidence of the closest space and the narrowest technical position. It is not advisable to use the roll, since the trill would involve an overly strong arm movement which would greatly curtail the position of the fingers and make it utterly impossible to render a trill in a clean manner. Because of this, the trill can be played with the fingers only. The execution of the trill is, therefore, a matter of finger gymnastics. Only in specific cases do we advise the roll as a support to the finger trill. Tetzel is justified in saying: "Thus we see that the roll is indispensable when the tension becomes too great, but we also see that the roll becomes insufficient and dispensable as the tension decreases. On the other hand, we notice that the active finger movement becomes more necessary and available." As a final deduction he quotes the opposite opinions of Bandmann and Breithaupt. Bandmann writes: "The trill is nothing more than a cooperative passive roll movement of the upper and lower arm." Breithaupt says: "The trill is an absolute 'non-finger matter,' a playing with quiet fingers, without any lifting and without false muscular contraction, a lateral shaking of a slightly tensed hollow hand." These ideas and opinions will not stand the test of time. They arouse false impressions.

The Pressure

In the previous chapters on Modes of Touch, we dealt with tone, which was produced by striking the key. This method was termed the "firm finger stroke." This stroke generally demands

109

that the striking finger should be raised above the key before the action takes place. We shall now view the mode of tone production which ensues when the finger touches the key prior to the pressure. The time of contact prior to this pressure touch naturally need only be very slight. Through this pressure the hammer is thrust against the strings. We should lay the fixed fingers on the keys in a curved position, letting the upper arm hang flexibly, bending the lower arm to the level of the keyboard and fixing the wrist suitably to the arm's length so that the muscles of the shoulder will carry the entire weight of the arm. By pressing down the key with the fixed finger we feel the weight of the arm resting upon said finger and also perceive that the arm remains passive.

The key pressure will bear many changes from minimum to maximum weight. The minimum weight must be heavy enough to cause the hammer to sway, while the maximum weight depends upon the strength of the player. The nerves in the finger-tips are a vital part of tone shading, especially in the application of pressure playing.

Pressure playing is by no means a modern invention. I refer to the succession of uniform *pianissimo* chords for which the teacher advises the pupils to lay their fixed fingers on the respective keys, pressing them down with equal strength, not permitting the fingers to leave the keys with each lift. The equally strong touch for the octave, third, fifth, etc., of a chord is accomplished much more easily in this way. In this case it is safer by far to use the pressure touch than to use the stroke from above.

Amateurs will find this aforementioned touch a great aid in avoiding the mistake of leaving out (or jumping over) chord tones, a result of uneven chord touch. It is self-evident that all of the rules already mentioned must be strictly obeyed with regard to the pressure touch.

The feeling of muscular release and muscular relaxation dare not be sacrificed. Muscular tension should not exceed the absolute measure needed in the art of pressure playing.

When rendering a singing tone, I deem it exceedingly important not to bend the fingers too much, but rather to straighten the fingers enough so that the flat part of the first joint of the finger instead of the finger-tip will rest upon the key. In this manner the delicate sensory nerves of the fingers come into their own, making it possible for the player to bring forth a large scale of rich tone colors. A pianist feels his way into this style of touch and with it he believes it possible to transfer his impressions to the piano directly.

General Hints on Touch

The above-mentioned modes of touch, plus mixtures, are applied in the countless technical problems. In part this mixing of modes depends upon the talent of the player. It may be a fact that the plain movements are *passé*, the mixed movements being suggested instead. For the most part, chords will endure a mixture of throw, stroke and swing; rapid runs will bear a thrust of the fingers and, more or less, the roll movement. Since each movement is a result of muscular work, it is imperative that every muscle engaged in the act of stroke and touch be strengthened through exercise. It was indeed an original but utterly wrong idea' of pedagogues to insist upon cutting out the active movement of the finger and designating only the equal fixation as a necessary means for the touch. The fingers are the members which serve as immediate means in the category of motion. The application of their inherent delicate feeling would become partly an illusory matter if we expected only fixation of them and disclaimed their intensive active efficacy.

In my opinion the development of fingers should be encouraged, since it is the point of departure in the attainment of a good keyboard technique. The student should be taught the fundamental principles of finger technique from the very beginning. Fixation and finger curvature may seem unimportant to him at first, because he is unable to appreciate the significance of future relative factors.

By means of continuous practice, the student will be able to control his fingers equally, strengthen them and to a certain degree, make them independent of one another. Of course, the third finger will always remain stronger and the fifth finger, due to its natural condition, weaker. Between these two is situated the so-called "sorrow child," the fourth or weak finger. This feeble member gives the beginner the most trouble when he attempts to equalize the tones of a run or a scale. Since it is the weakest of the fingers, it is treated with too much consideration. Here again, diligent practice is the only remedy. Players have a very bad habit of using the third instead of the fourth finger when playing thirds and sixths belonging to chords. For the sake of convenience, they constantly use the second and third fingers or the thumb and third finger when playing a trill, avoiding the third and fourth fingers whenever possible. The pupil who uses the fourth finger, whether it be in the trill or chord (or whenever possible), will gradually become accustomed to its application. He will thereby strengthen it to such a degree that the rendition of a trill (the fourth finger taking the first note) will be a performance of roundness and clearness, having made it more convenient for the functioning of the secondary or adjacent finger in the after-beat. The application of the fourth finger will finally become a matter of equality, which will not differ in strength from the rest of the fingers. (Refer to first book.)

In many cases pianists build solely upon technique. Such great artists as Reisenauer possess it to a high degree. A modern player must have the most polished finger technique at his command.

We have already spoken about the necessary calm and restfulness in the carrying out of the variable touch. Notwithstanding, the teacher's main concern should be the spasmodic stiffening of the joints which might be a result of this touch. A strong fixation is unavoidable in forte and fortissimo playing. But one should always think of relaxing the muscles whenever the opportunity arises, so that the fixation will be interrupted and lessened. As we have already stated, this relaxation must ensue from within, minus any noticeable movement.

The first lessons should not occupy the player's mind with arm movements. It should be discussed at a later moment. These movements (when playing a descending scale) are also applied to chord and scale work, as a lateral "going along," while swinging the hand over the fixed thumb by means of a rotation in the radius joint. With regard to the carrying out of finger technique for chord and scale playing, we refer you to the first book for more thorough and detailed explanations.

Next in order, with regard to the carrying out of chords and octave progressions, are the pressure and throw and the stroke and swing (refer to Etude, first book). The fixation of wrist and hand is an additional preliminary condition. Full-handed chords and octaves in themselves demand a greater tension of the fingers and hand, which might easily evoke fatigue. Therefore, if we employ the shoulder or elbow joint, the stronger arm and shoulder muscles will be called upon to carry out these features. These elementary rudiments guarantee a longer endurance and greatly delay fatigue. There are no doubt instances where the wrist is used to great advantage, wherefore the frist motion is practiced in octave studies. At all events the skilled pianist must be able to play chords and octaves in rapid succession from the shoulder, as well as from the elbow joint and wrist.

Posture While Playing

We have given the necessary instructions in our first book concerning sitting, body, arm, hand and finger position. They may serve the pupil as a standard in the study of touch, which leads to the controlling of fingers and the promotion of their independence. These exercises serve to strengthen the fingers and to develop the so-called knuckle stroke, where the player raises the fingers to a height of one inch and then lays them on the keys in the previously explained manner. Thereafter he practices the quick raising (up to an inch) of the individual fingers successively, without changing their curvature, keeping them stationary for a while and then dropping them without pressure. This exercise can be done in regular time, by counting rhythmically. The above movement should be carried out quickly, but in a slow tempo at first, the student counting several beats to a movement. This should be repeated until the movement is completely mastered. Little by little the tone will grow in accordance with the growth of energy the player has acquired through the throw and stroke, which causes the fingers to swing. After the individual fingers have accomplished this movement, it is time to practice the same exercise with two fingers in the following manner: Raise the first finger at the moment the second finger falls, repeating this exercise to a point of fluency and distinctiveness. Many pedagogues are of the opinion that a *leggiero* or a *nonlegato* is the common result of "finger playing." I do not agree with them on this point. Here is my argument. Whenever the energetic "striking finger" falls very rapidly from above and the opposite "lifting finger" raises itself at the same moment, it will take the damper so much time to fall that the *"legato"* will not suffer an interruption. On the other hand, a *legato* is accomplished through the pressure touch.

We now come to the principal mode of touch, the *legato*. We differentiate between the following modes of touch: the *legatq* *(leggiero)*, *legatissimo*, and further, the *staccato*, *portamento* and *nonlegato*.

Legato

Legato means the "tying together" of two notes, but excludes the "sounding together" in the joined consecutive single notes. For that reason the second tone must be issued clearly the moment the first tone is checked (by the damper). *Legato* playing is accomplished most perfectly and more easily by means of the pressure touch (compare first book, Inventions). But it is also possible by means of the knuckle stroke. The assertion, "that the *legato* which is produced by means of pressure causes the weight to be *pushed* from one finger to another," is based on fact. It has practically no significance, because in this pressure style and in the rapid tone progressions the essential work of the hand muscles will enter into the question of the attainment of the necessary and absolute equalization as well as the simplified and balanced rhythm.

The more one disclaims the physical weight in this mode of touch and the more one pushes muscle work and prompt release of fingers to the foreground, so much nearer will one approach the *leggiero* in running work. *Leggiero*, nicely carried out, is an excellent example of balanced technique. It is used abundantly.

Many players disclaim almost entirely the arm weight in the playing of *pianissimo* runs and expressly use the finger touch. We fully agree with Tetzel's opinion, when he writes: "Since we define 'finger technique' as the running motion of the fingers, which carry the heavily laden arm at liberty, so do we define 'weight technique' and 'finger technique' as closely allied factors. Both are elementary parts of the collective comprehension of piano technique, to which we add the roll and several other functions. The application of the arm weight in scale technique would be impossible should the fingers shun their duty. In this sense, finger technique is the primary function. Most likely finger technique is possible without the effect of arm weight." And I would add, "and its development is absolutely necessary."

The term *"legatissimo"* is greatly used. It indicates that the player should pay as much attention as possible to the connecting of tones. *Legatissimo* really means the holding of one note until two or more are played, thus causing a harmonious formation, as, for instance, in the smallest sound combination with syncopated pedalling.

Nonlegato, Portamento, Staccato

As we have already mentioned above, *nonlegato* is the antithesis of *legato*, the first being called disconnected "finger playing," accomplished by a timed lifting of the finger. When this lifting occurs after the damper has already checked the tone or before a new touch ensues, the *legato*, is out of question, the result being a *nonlegato*. If the "respiratory pause" is still greater between two notes, the *nonlegato* becomes a *portamento*, which is indicated by combined dots and slurs over the notes. *Portamento* means weighing the notes or leaning over the same. It is therefore generally used in quiet tone progressions, whereas the *nonlegato* is used as an utter measure of separation in the livelier progressions. As it takes a certain time for the damper to fall, these two modes are impractical in very quick runs, the *legato* style alone being possible.

Portamento and *nonlegato* playing are produced by means of the plain finger touch, the throw and swing from the wrist, the elbow or even the shoulder joint, and also through the pressure touch, in combination with the first "touch possibilities." While the *portamento* and *nonlegato* are a matter of tone separation without restriction of note values, the *staccato* is a mode of touch (apart from the separation in tone progressions) which effects a short duration of the tone in question. It is indicated by dots or vertical strokes over the notes, mostly quarters, eighths, etc. When these dots occur over greater valued notes, such as whole, halves, etc., their purpose serves to shorten the value of the respective notes. Thus we hold the notes only half as long as their nominal value. Since *staccato* calls for short and snappy playing, the above cannot be looked upon as *staccato* playing in the true sense. A *staccato* with fixed fingers emanates from the wrist, or possibly from the elbow and shoulder joint, this mode being very practical in octave and chord progressions. The finger *staccato* must also be practiced. An acute or extreme *staccato* is used very seldom. Ph. E. Bach tells his pupils to carry out a *staccato* on the instruments of that era, "as though one were playing on *redhot* keys."

The Uses of Touches for Technical Studies

It has already been said that the training of fingers is most essential in the primary grade of piano playing. To this end the five-finger exercises are basic in finger technique. These may be found in every "School of Piano Playing," for which reason I shall not express myself any further with regard to them. Little by little these finger exercises go beyond the five-tone range and advance to the octave by degrees, finally extending to several octaves. Through their application in all keys (major and minor) the upper clavicles (black keys) come into use, necessitating changes of finger positions, with which the pupils must acquaint themselves. At first they should be played *legato*. Eventually they will be of indispensable value in the advanced stage, a factor in the attainment of round and mellow tones. The *legato* pressure touch should be practiced to the greatest advantage in the playing of scales. Thirds are yet to be mentioned. These are to be played simultaneously. Both tones of these intervals should be struck with equal strength. Exercises involving one or more stationary fingers (they are such, wherein one or more fingers rest upon the keys) demand thorough consideration. Here strong concentration is advantageous. By avoiding all unnecessary movements and maintaining a quiet hand, the clean finger work will come into its own. Suppressing the stationary thumb while the rest of the fingers repeat a note is a practical preparatory exercise for *staccato* playing. For reiteration of the same tone (above all, rapid repetitions), the changing of fingers is advisable, although the same finger can strike the note repeatedly. Even the fixed finger can accomplish this through the swing of the relaxed hand or arm.

Breithaupt writes: "Changing of fingers as a particular technical element should be discontinued." Liszt, the father of the modern piano, was opposed to this idea. In fact, he prescribed the change of fingers in many places. The piano player of today must control the practice of "finger changing," as well as the "single-finger" repetition, and dare not disclaim either of the two.

Every pupil should pass an obligatory State Examination on scale studies after having studied music for a half year. All instruction on scale playing has already been given. Here we might add a few suggestions with regard to exercises on the passing "over" and "under" of the fingers.

Let us begin with the exercise of passing under the second finger and then follow with the third, fourth and fifth fingers. Looseness (or lightness) is a preliminary condition in good scale playing which does not exclude the independent finger style entirely. The "passing under" of fingers is facilitated through the inner position of the hand, purposed by the rotary movement of the radius joint. The degree of this "passing-under" movement is lessened through the self-evident proceeding of the hand.

Using the swing in this "passing over" procedure also calls for preliminary practice. In *fortissimo* scales the finger thrust is completed through pressure. In *arpeggios* (broken chords) this passing under and over of the fingers and arms is similar to that in scale playing, but in a wider degree. *Arpeggios* extending over two octaves and played in faster tempo are aided by the arm swing in the "over" and "under" passing. The lateral proceeding and the lifting and lowering (sinking) of the hand (eventually the arm) evolves a kind of wavy movement.

Octaves, Sixths, and Thirds

Octaves can be executed through plain finger work and if the fingers become fixed, they can be played from the wrist, from the elbow, as well as from the shoulder.

The former rule, playing them exclusively from the wrist, has always been taught but not always carried out. Octaves are played from the elbow more frequently, the wrist being somewhat fixed. *Fortissimo* octaves are usually played from the shoulder, although *pianissimo* octaves can be played in the same manner.

To claim that any of the above possibilities are useless in octave playing is decidedly wrong. Each mode can be applied adequately at the opportune time and must be controlled through practice.

The question as to whether or not we should begin the octave exercises with the *legato* or *staccato* is, generally speaking, a matter of indifference. But, owing to the leap (in octave playing), which causes most pupils much concern in *legato* playing, we prefer the *staccato* octaves as a preliminary means, especially for those players with small hands. The octave expansion (tension) demands a proportionately strong fixation for small hands. By playing octave progressions slowly, it is possible to relax the muscles after each octave rendition, thereby guarding against fatigue and stiffness. As the speed increases, the chance for relaxation becomes smaller, and when further acceleration takes place, relaxation becomes impossible. The fingers will then 'quickly become tired, making it utterly impossible to continue, since all the muscles engaged in the act of playing will become cramped. Therefore, a long continuance of rapid octave progressions is not at all practicable. In Liszt's Sixth Rhapsody such octaves extend through several pages. Most players become fatigued before long when playing this composition and only the most skilled pianists are able to carry on, since this already difficult task becomes more intricate through dynamic intensification. There is no remedy which will alleviate this condition, save the possible physical release, in other words, the relaxation of muscles and the greater demand upon the stronger muscles of the upper arm and shoulder. This remedy may not be a permanent cure, but it will at least delay the painful condition. In this case, the wrist *staccato* is eliminated almost entirely. The leverage movement is so slight that little by little a vibration, or vertical shaking, will take place.

Many players raise and lower the wrist whenever a short release of the tension is required. The octave section in the last movement of Beethoven's Sonata Op. 53 is frequently played by *virtuosi* in the said *vibrato* style, most likely being perceived as *glissando-octaves*.

However, these vibratory octaves are seldom applied, whereas *staccato* octaves and those played by means of thrusting the entire weight masses of arm and hand, and also the swing and stroke, occur far more frequently. These are the so-called *martellato* or hammer-blow octaves. We admonish the players not to throw the hand back too far or too strongly when using the wrist stroke for octave playing, since restraint and stiffness might easily ensue. We advise them not to employ the wrist motion for octaves, except for short, springy octave successions. In the playing of *legato* octaves, the gliding of the thumb and little finger is an essential factor. Absolute *legato* octaves for one hand alone are almost excluded, since they (in the case of small hands) can be played with the thumb, and fifth finger only. Where large hands are concerned, the thumb must always glide, leaving the *legato* work entirely to the fourth and fifth fingers. (Refer to first book.)

Gliding exercises are exceedingly important for *legato* octaves. Sliding the thumb or the fifth finger from a higher key to a lower one is easy, but this is not so in reverse, since more skill is required. The partial engaging of the fourth finger (in octave playing) should

116

occur only where the hand is able to expand beyond the octave. Chromatic octaves should (because of the uniform position of the hand) be played with the thumb and fifth finger, without the lateral movement, wherein great skill can be acquired through practice in the attainment of the *legato*. In the playing of octaves, it is advisable to strike more heavily with the little finger than with the thumb, since the little finger of the right hand frequently accentuates the melodic tone. In the left hand this finger nearly always must mark the bass.

The carrying out of consecutive *legato* sixths conditions an almost uninterrupted application of the rotary movement of the wrist and lower arm. The successive fingering $\frac{4\,5}{1\,2}$ alone necessitates a relaxation of both hand and arm, which, at the recurrence of the $\frac{4}{1}$, evolves a strong movement, especially in the ascension. Should the thumb carry out a gliding movement, the above movement will be reduced. But even then the *legato* will extend itself to the fourth and fifth fingers only.

In general the *staccato* sixths are carried out in the same manner as are the *staccato* octaves. The tension of fingers with regard to *legato* sixths $\frac{4\,5}{1\,2}$ is very great. Hence it follows that fatigue takes place quickly. For example, take Chopin's so-called "Sixths-Etude," which demands great endurance of the player. Here every opportunity must be used for relaxation of the muscles.

The carrying out of thirds also lays claim to certain methods in finger technique, a direct procedure, which calls upon only the swing of the wrist and support of the arm. An absolute *legato* is possible only where the occasion does not demand a change of hand position, as in the fingering $\frac{4\,5\,4\,5}{2\,1\,2\,1}$ etc. Such fingering is hardly applicable in the quicker *legato* third scales. However, when ascending, the second, third, fourth and fifth fingers can continue the *legato*, except that the thumb might disturb the *legato* somewhat in gliding from key to key. But such shortcomings can be overcome through practice and skill, so that a sparkling "third scale" is eventually achieved. When descending, the fifth finger must pass over the adjacent member, which again will cause a hiatus or gap. Nevertheless, with skillful execution, the uniformity can be maintained, the slight deviations being scarcely audible. The third finger dare not be held down too long when the fifth finger is about to pass over it, in order that the flow remain undisturbed. It must not be held down for too short a length of time, however, or else the tone, played by the third finger, will sound as though it were torn off, thereby blemishing the *legato*. Thirds should be practiced with one hand alone until the pupil has mastered the above. It often happens that the third finger (as indicated in said exercise) is often omitted entirely when consecutive thirds are played in quicker tempi, especially when both hands play in thirds. For "trills in thirds" to which the fingering $\frac{4\,5\,4\,5}{2\,1\,2\,1}$, can be applied, we regard a vertical shaking of the hand

(eventually arm) as a secondary means for the prevention of fatigue.
As a general rule, chords are played by means of throw, stroke and swing of the fixed fingers, emanating from the wrist or shoulder joint. The fixation of fingers ensues in the following manner: The tips of the striking fingers should lie level, projecting over the others. In the quick exchange of chords refixing of all members must ensue with lightning-like quickness.

Chords ensuing from the elbow joint are used quite frequently, and the rhythmics therefrom are regulated by the swing and pressure. Uniform accompaniment chords are carried out advantageously in the following manner: laying the fixed fingers on the keys, then striking the same through a uniform pressure (refer to first book). The disproportionate quality of chord tones often goes so far that certain individual tones sometimes are missing, especially when one strikes blindly at a remote bass tone. Some pupils do not take notice of these gross mistakes, especially, when the pedal conceals the shortcoming. Very often the final chord is "ripped off" ahead of the remote bass tone and is contrasted with the preceding chords of uniform value in a faulty manner, either through an overly soft touch or a heavy bang. This faulty touch is so widespread that we advise pupils to avoid it.

Chords which are rendered by means of pressure can be dynamically well regulated. The feeling in the finger tips makes it possible to render the softest *pianissimo* and an even *"crescendo* to *forte"*; and *vice versa*, "loud" to gradually "soft." Contrary to this, loud chords frequently demand the throw, eventually the arm stroke from the elbow, and finally the shoulder joint with fairly strong fixation of the wrist and fingers.

Self-evidently, we must sometimes deliver wrist chords. But their application should be reserved for rare cases, for reasons already mentioned.

It is difficult to accentuate individual notes of a chord played with the same hand, as, for instance, the marking of a melody which is harmonized in the same hand. The main burden rests upon the fingers that have to play the melody. It is advisable to extend the extreme tip of the respective finger over the plane which is arranged by the fixed chord fingers when bringing a tone into prominence. In this way the tone will come forth somewhat stronger when the key is struck. But it will also sound ahead of the others. The pre-sounding of these notes, however, must be so slight that it does not become too obvious. It is obligatory that the accompaniment be played softer than the melody. When one practices, it is best to exaggerate these differences and divide the proportionate loudness through strictest ear control (refer to first book).

Touch for Polyphonic Playing and for Phrasing Parts

Polyphony (plurality of voices) is a musical setting in which a number of independent voices (parts) are carried out in the course of a musical composition. These voices are all entitled to equal significance and in similar manner, therefore, alternately bring

118

forth the themes and counterpoints. Entry and progression with regard to each voice must be clear and distinguishable. Great difficulties ensue with regard to touch, especially in the organized cadences of *strettos* and *codettas*, in which the thematic entrances of voices immediately follow one another. The performance of such sections has been essentially treated in the preceding chapter (accentuation of individual tones in chord work of the single hand). All aforesaid modes of touch can be applied to the entry of a phrase and the dynamical shading of its climax. We also might mention the respective touch of the phrase's cadence, which often requires a respiratory pause and an occasional "drawing off"—or even a "fading out." Ofttimes the last tone of a phrase is the weakest. In some instances its note value is somewhat reduced. This is accomplished by means of thrusting the fingers, or through a "drawing off" of the same, over the keys. Even the tone which is situated on the strong beat must sometimes be drawn off unaccentuated. The composer will always indicate in one way or another if there is a need for special accentuation of the note in question. One should use utmost precaution when ending phrases, so that the last tone does not appear broken off or unintentionally loud, or remain unheard by untrained ears.

VI. PHRASING

Phrasing means fixing the limits of phrases and their nuances. These are more or less closely involved inherent members of musical ideas. Musical phrasing is indicated through use of specific signs, such as slurs, *fermates* (pauses), and commas (,), all conceived as a means of breaking, marking the start and finish of phrases, being distinguished through dynamical shading.

Phrasing Marks in the Notation

Composers employ almost entirely the phrasing-bows for the joining of phrases. These bows are similar in form to the *legato* slurs. For that reason one is taken for the other, both looking alike. The application of these bows has many shortcomings. For the sake of orientation a great number of phrasing signs were issued, in fact too many. This overabundance of symbols caused many players to lose sight of the most essential ones.

In order to facilitate matters, these *legato*-bows were again partly dispensed with, thereby making it a common rule to play all notes *legato* unless the *staccato*-dots demanded otherwise, the bows representing "phrasing-bows" exclusively.

Whenever the end of one phrase and the beginning of a new one fell on one and the same note, two cross slurs were applied.

⌢
ſ When it was necessary to hold the closing note of a phrase for its full value, the end of the slur (bow) was joined with the beginning of the new one (⌢ſ); or a dash (tenuto) (—) was placed over the note.

As an indicator for an interrupted entrance into a new phrase, many writers applied the interrupted bow (⊣⊢) in order to make the structure more clear to the eye.

At the endings of the chief divisions two small strokes (∥) were used occasionally; for subdivisions one small stroke (∕) was employed. Commas (,) also made this structural phrasing more definite.

For discrimination between heavy and light bars the signs (Υ) for heavy, (Υᴵ) for light were chosen. Now and then the bar lines were punctuated at the beginning of light measures.

So much for the orientation in the application of musical phraseology.

Phrasing in the Art of Interpretation

For the recognition of phrases not distinctly characterized a knowledge of musical forms is essential.*

---

*Details on this subject can be found in books on Phrasing, by Hugo Riemann.

VII. THE PEDAL

Very often, when analyzing new piano works (while giving a lesson), I became convinced that my matured pupils were unable to *tread time* when using the pedal. This blunder was made by pupils (who studied under other tutors before they came to me) at successful concerts, the audience taking no offense at such pedalling and the critics making no note of it. This again proves how important it is to train the musical ear to hear such mistakes. Whenever I told such a pupil to "tread time," he would raise his foot on the "strong beat," immediately lowering it again.

This post-treading (treading after) is generally called "syncopated pedalling," the opposite of "time-treading."

I have tried in every possible way to teach the otherwise excellent pianist how to tread time, so that the foot tread comes together with the touch of the heavy beat. Time-treading is a style of pedalling which the player should utilize more often. Many instructors teach only the syncopated pedalling. For that reason, most players have become accustomed to the syncopated style of treading and have gradually forgotten the time-reading; in fact, they have taken the latter for incorrect pedalling. It requires a certain skill to tread precisely on the first time unit so that there is no remnant (possibly caused by an unprecise touch) of the preceding measure sounding (or hanging over) into the ensuing one. Generally, the harmony changes on the strong beat, the bass tone sounding with the harmony and serving as a foundation upon which the harmonic structure is formed. All of Beethoven's Sonatas can be properly pedalled by means of the time-tread. The same can be applied to Chopin's compositions. When playing "Beethoven," it is better to hold the pedal for a shorter length of time. When playing "Chopin," a greater time length is advisable, since, in the latter, the tone progressions must very often swim in the so-called "pedal vapor," while in the case of Beethoven, transparency is the law of delivery.

You have already seen in the preliminary lines that too little stress is generally laid upon pedal technique. Just as we attempt to render the note values exactly, so must the touch of the foot be practiced deliberately until it can be accomplished subconsciously, so to say. Once we have acquired enough technique to render a composition fairly well, it is also advisable to study foot technique with greatest accuracy.

For the "treading-down" of the pedal, it is advantageous to sit in a favorable position, in other words, it is advisable to place the feet so that the heels are firmly set on the floor, while the forepart (the ball inclusive) of the feet rests on the pedals. It is important to keep the feet in close contact with the pedals while playing so

All parts or members of musical ideas which are sectionally divided are either time motives or time groups, semi-movements or periods.

Time motives are short progressions, which have only *one* heavy time unit.

Time groups are tone progressions which have two heavy time units as a collective unity.

Semi-movements are four *time motives*, consisting of collective tone progressions, whose main accent lies on the heavy time unit of the second group.

Periods are composed of an antecedent (first phrase) and a consequent (second phrase).

Sonata in G-major, by L. van Beethoven, Op. 49, No. 2 (2nd movement).

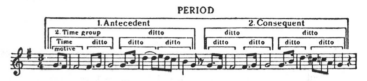

The *subdivided* motives demand special attention with regard to phrasing. These are short motives in which a single time unit forms a central point, so that there are as many possible central points as there are time units at hand. (For instance, Beethoven, Sonata Op. 2, No. 1, Allegro, measures 26 to 33.)

Sonata in G-major, by L. van Beethoven, Op. 31, No. 1, Rondo.

As phrased in Cotta Edition:

More logical:

How can we improve the phrasing when the notation of a composer leaves us in doubt? How can we determine the end and central point of a phrase in order to properly render the same?

The end of a phrase, in regard to the harmony, can be either a full cadence, half cadence or deceptive cadence. In the so-called "closes," where a feminine cadence can follow (that is, when the final note falls on a light beat of a measure), the "close" of a phrase is evident.

Extreme points are effected through *lengths* on the *heavy* beats of a measure (so long as the harmonization does not demand a continued melodic flow) and may be followed by a feminine cadence.

Pauses and rests also occasion a figure (form); here the ending of a phrase can for the most part be easily determined, provided that the rests do not serve as a shortening of the notes.

The end of a phrase is also distinguishable through the form of the commencing time motion, which can be entered upon with or without an up-beat. (Bach, 1. Two-part Invention.) Should the time motive contain an up-beat, then the separation (or the articulate structure) will be found where the up-beat recurs. This, of course, disappears occasionally (for instance, Prelude in D-major, by Bach).

If the time motive commences on the heavy beat, the phrase in question usually faces one of similar structure (Sonata by Beethoven, Op. 2, No. 3, Opening; or Op. 110, 2nd movement).

Through this confronting of similar structures, the fixed limitation is thus marked: Similarly separates, dissimilarity binds.

Symmetries are very often alike, yet disturbances can occur, as follows:

1. Through insertions or extensions. These ensue,
   (a) through sequences. They are motives, transferred to other degrees of the scale, subordinating the harmony. They occur most often in the additional movement (Beethoven, Sonata Op. 57, final movement, Presto; Andante F-major—eight measures instead of fourteen; Phantasy Op. 77, Allegro con brio);
   (b) through repetition or alteration of the second heavy link, which serve as improved cadences, transitions or confirmed final closes (Beethoven, Sonata in E-flat major Op. 27, 3rd movement, 25th measure; Op. 26, theme; Op. 22, Adagio).
2. Through omissions, mostly originating from the unification of two phrases (Beethoven, Sonata F-major Op. 10 No. 2, 3rd movement, Presto).

Separations (in the carrying out of melodies) are marked by leaps and skips, which interrupt the essential melodic flow, indeed, many times by change of direction in the tone progressions.

Repetition of tones also plays an occasional part in the organization of articulate tone links.

Dynamic shading and the applicable "agogic" alteration is most essential in the delivery of phrases if one is to recognize the start and finish of a phrase. The rule is that every phrase should have *only one* dynamical climax, and that it should always appear as the heavy note in one of the time motives, time groups, etc., according to the aforesaid explanation. In general, the climax is brought about through a *crescendo*, being followed by a *diminuendo*; on the other hand, phrases starting on the down-beat sometimes swell into a climax, without the requirement of a diminution from this point.

For the agogic alterations, namely the slight time alterations, which the composer does not indicate and which are left to the good judgment and taste of the player, the general rule, "that a certain acceleration should lead up to a climax," is of value, while the climax note experiences a slight prolongation. From there on a retardation frequently takes place, continuing to the final note of a phrase.

The embracement and separation of consecutive phrases is shown when the latter comes to an ultimate close through a pause. But the problem becomes more intricate in the case of uninterrupted successions of phrases. A break must occur between such phrases. It must not be short and abrupt as it will interrupt the fluency and thereby cause the entire musical structure to sound choppy.

The final note of the first phrase is usually not stressed. The first note of the new phrase must predominate somewhat or, as is often the case in Beethoven's works, it culminates with *fortissimo* and the new attack immediately resounds in *pianissimo*. Under certain circumstances, this aforesaid separation (or break) is produced through an unessential prolongation of the final note. One must have great foresight in organizing the subdivisible motives or eventually separating them, as here there is an imminent danger of delivering the motives in a detached and affected manner.

Reimann uses this sign (⌐¬) for the limitation of phrases. Others prefer a small (/) or large (**/**) stroke at the end of a phrase. The large stroke signifies the separation of two phrases. In the case of the *legato*, this separation is brought about through an adequate pause (such as is used by singers for taking breath); in the *staccato* or *portamento*, through a dynamically strong attack when entering into the new phrase. The semi-stroke is used in the *legato* when the weaker separation occurs through a corresponding shading (namely, a fading of the end note) in the preceding phrase, and a predomination of the first note in the new phrase. This stroke is not used in the *legato* when the weaker separation occurs through a release of the hand (respiratory pause). In the *staccato* and *portamento* phrases, the weaker separation is brought about through a lighter attack when entering into the new phrase. Should the final note of a phrase represent the first note of the ensuing phrase, then the stroke (/) is placed over or under the note, in which case the note is considered a "new phrase" entry. It is customary to u a stronger attack in such cases.

In the above we have briefly explained the origin and charac of phrases. In our opinion we have offered the pianist a means which he can determine a start, finish and climax, even though t is the danger that the inexperienced and dependent musician m be led astray, or, as Scharwenka says, "that such 'dissections' cause the student to lose sight of the musical climax." Appre ing phrases is not always a simple matter. The pupil eas comes confused at times and therefore requires the guidan teacher.

as to avoid the disturbing noise which is easily caused by their impact.

It is practical to acquire the technique of time-treading and syncopated pedalling by studying suitable passages, before engaging oneself in the working out of pedal employment in a musical composition.

The player should also practice the following exercise: Employ the pedal prior to the finger touch, for instance, as in the case of the appoggiaturas (grace notes), which must continue as bass notes. Employing the pedal in this manner is very difficult. It demands extreme concentration, because the foot touch must occur independent of and before the hand stroke. This anticipation note is also very important as a preliminary note to the entry of motives, since it must stand out sonorously from the very beginning. When we tread the pedal before the finger touch, the strings will vibrate somewhat without being struck, and the touch (tone) will be more lasting. Not until one has tried these preliminary exercises will it pay to engage in the ensuing research pertaining to the application of the pedals.

The modern pianos have two (sometimes three) pedals. The one to the right is called the "amplifier"; the one to the left is called the "diminisher."

The common terms for both pedals are as follows: right, "loud pedal" left, "soft pedal". The one to the right is also called the "damper pedal."

We shall first view the loud pedal, frequently referring to the accurate book of Louis Köhler, "The Pianoforte Pedal, its Nature and Artistic Application." In the first place, this book furnished a discussion on the pedal questions and was almost conclusive in its details. Unfortunately, it has been out of print for thirty years and cannot be added to our musical library as a study reference.

Instructions on the employment of the pedal are very difficult, as the rules upon which we base our support can scarcely be produced. The exceptions would most likely surpass the rules. In many cases one could play as well without the pedal as with the pedal, giving sound reasons for the carrying out of either method. Both modes may have their esthetic qualifications, and may be thoroughly effective. Very often, too, many places are pedalled differently by various artists, the diverging conceptions bearing no ill effects upon the musical parts. However, one dare not use the pedals carelessly or without consideration. Piano players who make a mere "foot rest" of the pedal and who lift their feet only when the conglomeration of tones becomes too great are far from being exponents of beautiful music.

The pedal raises the effects in musical renditions and is, therefore, an important and very often an indispensable auxiliary means. If good musicians of the past imagined they could get along without the pedal, it was due to their ignorance of pedal management, or else it was the fault of the poorly developed pedal mechanism.

Our next task will be a careful examination of pedal effects, to decide how and when to use the pedal. We shall have to confine ourselves to tone progressions to which the pedal cannot be applied and others for which the pedal must be used to advantage. The auxiliary means of pedalling (in accordance with signatures) is ofttimes a failure, since many composers use them for mere intimation. The customary signatures: (℔) for the down tread and (✱) for the release, take up too much space as accurate indicators of entry and close, since the pedal, when held down a moment longer than necessary, will cause a disturbing effect. When it is applied too late, a perceptible interruption takes place. More definite and easily determined signatures are indicated in the following style: (∟) for the beginning, (⌐) for the end, (+) for the quick change. Unfortunately they have never been adopted. We shall frequently utilize these signs in the ensuing treatise because of their brevity.

Louis Köhler indicates the duration of the pedals by placing a note on a staff line. Naturally, in this way he is able to designate the exact value of time. The carrying out of this pedal treatise would become too complicated should we touch upon the abundant treads in use. For that reason an exhaustive treatise would be impracticable.

A knowledge of pedal effects and careful ear control will gradually make us sensitive to pedalling. It will likewise prepare us to apply the pedals tastefully and unhesitatingly when playing at sight. Since the ear must decide in this case, it is imperative that we do all that is in our power to develop its training.

The mechanism of the pedal is brought into action by means of a lever, which lifts the dampers off the entire strings whenever the foot treads on the pedal, the dampers falling back when the foot is raised. On the other hand, when a key is struck (the pedal remaining idle), only the damper of the string which was struck will be lifted, so that only *one* string or *three uniform tones* (three strings tuned alike) will sound simultaneously. These strings will cease to sound the moment the finger leaves the key, since the damper has fallen on them again. Should we lift the entire dampers (by a pedal tread) and then strike a single tone, this specific tone will become enlarged through the simultaneous vibrating of the remaining strings, which have been liberated by the dampers. Tones sounding into one another, as well as the augmentation of power, can be effected beautifully by the skillful management of the pedal. On the other hand, if the pedal is mismanaged, it will produce ugly conglomerations.

The pedal is most effective in the bass, since the bass strings vibrate much longer than the upper ones. The high treble strings are least affected by the pedal, since their short vibrations do not necessitate much checking; in fact, the shortest strings do not possess any dampers, yet the pedal effect is noticeable here when the bass strings furnish a vibratory support.

We shall treat the pedal from three different viewpoints:

1. Its use in the attainment of tone volumes;

2. Its aid in the combining of single tones and chords which cannot be accomplished by the fingers;

3. Its use in the attainment of esthetic tonal effects, brought about by the predominance of individual tones and parts of a composition.

The third point of view is very often the result of the first two.

1. Utilizing the Pedal in the Attainment of Tone Volumes

We shall first refer to the *chord* progressions and thereafter to the *scale* progressions.

Application of the Pedal for Chord Progressions

In the playing of tones which belong to the same chord, prolonged pedalling will not produce dissonances; in other words, they will not be objectionable to the ear, regardless of whether we play simultaneous or broken chords.

Should the composer propose massive sound effects by means of accumulating chord tones, as, for instance, in Beethoven's Sonata in C-sharp minor, Op. 27, No. 2, 3rd movement:

or Beethoven's Sonata in C-sharp minor, Op. 27, No. 2, 3rd movement:

the "prolonged pedal" is necessary. Of course, here the ear must decide whether or not an occasional "dampening" or "checking" may be of value in preventing too great an accumulation of tone masses.

As an example of such effects (Köhler calls them "filling up" or "noise" effects) we offer the fragment from Chopin's Polonaise in C-sharp minor, Op. 26, No. 1.

It is advisable not to use the pedal at all times (even when the harmonic progressions permit it), since in many cases the phrasing might be impaired, the accumulation of sound might become too great, or the melodic flow be rendered indistinctly. Although there is no danger of dissonances running together in this case, *good judgment* should nevertheless be our constant watchword. It is obvious that melodic chord tones will sound harmoniously conjunctive during the pedal action. This may at times cause the melody to become inarticulate. Of course, after the tone is struck, it quickly decreases to such an extent that the ensuing note will drown it out; thus the melodic lead remains distinguishable. Notwithstanding this, it is advisable to lift the pedal quite often for the sake of clearness.

Sometimes one can tell when to change the pedal by the manner in which a figure is accented (for metrical and rhythmical accents the "new tread" is effective) or by the way a group is phrased, as,

for instance:    Here, most likely,

we would "pedal" as indicated. Now and then this is essential, since the tone position causes a natural tendency to *tread down* on the higher note, which can bear more pedalling than the lower note. Consecutive arpeggios, especially, are used abundantly as *accompanying figures.* Every model or form which comprises the notes of an individual chord will require a new pedal tread; whether or not this can be carried out in every instance is a matter which concerns the coherence of harmony and melody, the latter to be considered as the chief factor. So you see, the melody dare not suffer through the harmony, and yet both must take a "clean" effective part collectively. Following are a few examples (of Köhler), borrowed from musical literature, which will illustrate the permissible uses of the pedal:

Mozart, Sonata in C-major, 1st movement.

The first measure contains melody and accompanying notes, all belonging to one chord, which permit the prolongation of the pedal; the melodic tones also allow this prolongation, since they ascend and will not cover one another. In the second measure the "dominant-seventh" chord will bear a pedal tread, but for the sake of clearness, it should not be prolonged any further than the first c of the melody, which is unessential to the harmony. The second c again permits a *short* tread, which tends to announce the end of the phrase more definitely. In the third measure we find two groups based on the sub-dominant and tonic triads. Both of these call for a separate tread. The first two melody tones of the fourth measure belong to the "dominant-seventh" harmony, for which one tread is sufficient, since the f and g, when sounding together in the melody, will not be influenced by the repeated g of the trill. Because of the harmonic change, the melody tone e calls for a new pedal tread, which, owing to the phrasing, should not exceed the value of the respective note. Even though Mozart has not indicated the pedal at this point, it will be a great aid in "bringing out" the singing tone in this melody. A pedal effect such as this will be greatly supported by the full, round tones of our modern piano (an instrument which, of course, was unknown to Mozart), and, for esthetic reasons, its use will seem justifiable. It would be foolish to desist from such advantages (which serve to beautify a composition) just because Mozart was unaware of them. We would then play Bach's piano compositions on the clavicembalo (harpsichord) instead of the piano, since the aforesaid beautiful effects, brought about by means of stops and couplers on Bach's instrument (the forerunner of the piano), would be reason enough for us to disregard the piano. Were we to play Mozart's music as he himself heard it, we would have to choose the clavichord to accomplish this. Therefore, it is logical that we take advantage of every possible means to beautify music when playing on our modern piano.

The following illustration gives us an idea as to how harmonious figures should be pedalled:

Mozart, Sonata in F-major, 1st movement.

It is advisable to refrain from pedalling in the fifth measure, since the three melody tones should produce a harmonious effect. In the event of pedalling the "f" would too greatly cover the "a".*

Thus far we have viewed the utilization of pedals from the standpoint of chord progressions. It should seem natural to any experienced pianist to raise the pedal promptly enough (prior to the new chord entry) so as to avoid a "hanging over" of the preceding

---

*As is seen in the above illustration, there is a possibility of pedalling, but it seems as though its application (as indicated) is exaggerated. In the matter of style and good taste it is not practical. Today eminent pianists play "Mozart" very effectively without pedals. Very often a striking resemblance to pedalling is accomplished by means of extreme sustenuto touch.

chord into the ensuing one. Take, for example, the first movement
of Beethoven's Sonata in C-sharp minor, Op. 27, No. 2:

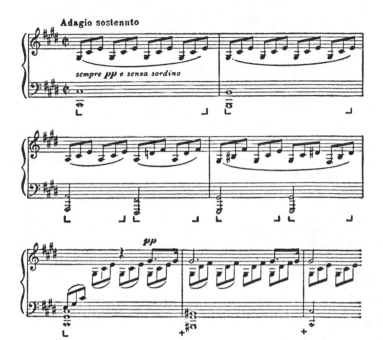

Here Beethoven has prescribed the pedalling throughout the
entire movement. The player should strictly observe the quick
"tread" and "release" at every change of chord from beginning to
end. In view of these quick changes, one should bear in mind that
any interruption, regarding the character of sound, will stand out
conspicuously and strike the ear disagreeably. We shall further
touch upon the character of sound when we come to the chapter on
"Esthetic Apportionment by Means of Pedals." Beethoven ex-
presses himself respectively in the following sentence: "Si deve
suonare tutto questo pezzo delicatissimamente e senza sordino."
It means that the movement should be played without dampers, in
other words, the pedal should be used in a manner which will not
permit the dampers to touch the strings.

Pupils who have studied harmony to some extent should have
very little trouble in using the pedals for chord progressions, but,
on the other hand, when playing single notes (by degrees), they
will be confronted with many intricacies. Sequential tones can
easily be blurred by the pedal, and yet very often, such graded tones
quite urgently demand pedalling, if the delivery is not to sound too
dry. Here judicious management will do much toward awakening
the soul of the instrument. We shall take the second part of

Chopin's Funeral March for example. (From Sonata in B-flat minor, Op. 35, 3rd movement.)

Here the tread is prolonged throughout the entire measure. Most likely, though, the adjacent notes (f, e-flat) of the melody are taken with one tread (pedal vapor), firstly, so as to permit the fundamental tone of the bass to "fill in" with the chord tones, and secondly, to avoid a break in the essential notes when releasing the pedal (with regard to the harmonious notes in the bass). We should bear the above in mind for the sake of uninterrupted melody and its character of sound. For instance, if we were to use a tread for four melodic tones alone (without the pedalled bass), they would become an unpleasant mixture of sound. But in conjunction with the harmonic bass tones, this melodic thread would produce a sonorous effect through its soft, yet full, tones. How shall we explain this? Only through the desired feeling for harmony. In the first place, our ear perceives the d-flat major-triad. The unessential notes (g-flat and e-flat) of the melody will not disturb the general harmonic impression, since they do not continue for long, and because their dissonant sound will disappear entirely when opposed to the strong feeling for the triad.

The above remarks should convince us that successive tonal degrees will bear pedalling very well, provided that the harmony absorbs the dissonances, which inevitably arise in the melodic structure. The dynamical degree of a tone decreases immediately following the touch, so that a preceding tone will (compared to the ensuing tone which appears "bodily" at the moment of touch) seem like a shadowy object. Should we attempt to play such unessential, inharmonious tones on the organ (where every tone comes forth equally strong), a chaos of sounds would arise.

We shall now scrutinize the "how" and "when" of scale pedalling and, in view of the same, follow Louis Köhler's instructions and his order of thoughts. For theoretical reasons he treated the *diatonic* and *chromatic* scales separately. All successive tones or degrees, with regard to relative scales or imaginable harmonies, are either chord tones or passing notes.

Passing notes are either diatonic notes belonging to the key in question or notes foreign to harmony, in other words, "chromatic tones."

Application of the Pedal for Diatonic Scale Progressions

All tones of the scale yield to consonances, with the exception of the mediant. The superdominant harmony of c-major, for instance, is g, b, d, f, a. Thus c is also on the fifth of the dominant chord (namely d, f, a, c) and is therefore harmoniously natural. Only the third (mediant) "e" will not permit a harmonic connection with the remaining tones, although it is a constituent part of the tonic triad. One can be easily convinced of this by playing the following notes:

If, for any reason, the pedal should be applied for diatonical progressions, 1, 2, - - - - 4, 5, 6, 7 degrees (every degree excepting the third) will be less sensitive and less disturbing in simultaneous harmonization, since they are harmonically suited to each other. We also might add that the semi-tones are more sensitive, when pedalling, than the whole tones. If we were to play a *scale with pedal*, the following would be a practical manner of pedalling:

When executing rapid scales, it is necessary at times to use fewer pedal treads, eventually only a single tread. It is possible to play a *glissando* with uninterrupted pedalling. As an example of scales of several octaves' range with one pedal tread, the g-minor run at the close of Chopin's Ballad in g-minor will be of value. We should observe how the pedal is to be raised promptly on the last fundamental tone. In doing this, we thus have the impression of a full-toned scale, and before our ear has time to perceive the dissonant harmonies, the pedal has already been raised so that only the feeling for the original key remains, the mixture of consonances and passing notes causing no disturbance.

If the pedal is used with modulated runs or "passages with pedal," one must also change the tread whenever a modulation takes place, regardless of the change which is necessary within the aforesaid key. The student with insufficient knowledge of harmony must rely upon the ear and change the pedal more often. Should the pedal be used for every feasible scale and passage? Of course not. Discretion should go hand in hand with procedure. We should first consider the character of a subject as well as the intention of the composer. In many instances he may only intimate the application of the pedal, thereby giving reasonable advise as to its feasibility.

Slower scale progressions demand a more frequent change of pedal.

Application of the Pedal for Chromatic Scale Progressions

Chromatic tone progressions can imply harmonic modulations. If, for any reason, such tone progressions demand pedalling, the pedal should also be changed when a change of key takes place.

Chromatic tone progressions can, moreover, be non-harmonic passing notes. We have already emphasized that two prolonged semi-tones are more sensitive than the whole tones when the pedal is used. When speaking of chromatic tones, we deal with semi-tones, those which have no relation to each other. As we already know, c is not relative to c-sharp with regard to "key" or "scale," although c-sharp is a derivative of c, according to our note system. Therefrom we shall conclude that it is best to refrain from pedalling when two chromatic tones are to be played. In spite of this, we often approve of pedalling when executing chromatic passages.

In the case of unaccentuated chromatic tone progressions, the pedal can be applied very often without a disturbing effect, as, for instance, when such semi-tones interrupt the melody supported by solid harmony; in other words, when the dissonances thus produced are absorbed by the dominating harmonious chord. Very short treads are often possible in tone positions where the bass or intermediate position must be treated more carefully than the treble. The dynamic degree of these tone positions also plays an essential part in pedalling. Delicate *pianissimo* embellishments in the higher positions will bear pedalling, even in the event of accumulated chromatic progressions. For instance, Chopin's florid work calls for continuous pedalling. Even two or more simultaneous chromatic tone progressions are imaginable in conjunction with solid chords which are occasionally pedalled. Considering the height of positions, the accumulated dissonances thereby demand extreme precaution.

Occasionally an "organ point" must be sustained by means of the pedal. For instance, the left hand will sound the bass, the pedal sustaining the same through a series of chords. As it is essential for this tone to sound through the chords, any entanglement arising from chromatic tone progressions must be accepted as unavoidable, the composer being held responsible for said effect.

In order to again sum up the results of our study of the application of the pedal and its influence upon diatonic and chromatic tone progressions, we, in conclusion, repeat the aforesaid: "The application of the pedal is possible when the dissonances thus produced are absorbed by the harmony; in other words, when the feeling for a definitely distinguishable harmony is ever prevalent."

2. Application of the Pedal in Attaining Legato Effects which Are Impossible with Fingers Alone

Application of the Pedal for Uniform Chords in Various Positions

We frequently come across sections in piano literature which should evidently sound connected. This, however, is impossible for small hands where great expansions occur in this branch of "keyboard technique." It is only logical that even normal or average fingers are unable to reach or bind widely spanned notes, such as broken accompaniment figures. Here the bass tone is situated about two octaves distant from chords which should continue to sound with the said bass note. That such sections are easily joined by means of the pedal and that they demand such procedure should be clear to every player.

Chords belonging to the same harmony (in different positions) for which it is necessary to use the same fingers consecutively, cannot be played legato without the aid of the pedal. The gaps which arise from such fingering may, of course, be somewhat lessened by the *gliding* and *sliding* of the fingers. In spite of this, these gaps cannot be bridged. They disappear entirely with proper pedal management, as, for instance, in Symphonic Etudes, Theme, by R. Schumann.

Pedalling Chords which Are Harmonically Different

In order to bind chords which are harmonically different, it is best to use the syncopated pedal. Syncopated pedalling is rendered in the following manner: Prolong the pedal a moment beyond the touch of the ensuing chord, thereupon raising and dropping the foot. Theoretically, this mode of syncopated pedalling may be objectionable, but practically, it will meet with approval. When using the syncopated pedal, both (preceding and ensuing) chords will discordantly run together for a moment. But before the player is actually aware of this discordance, the first chord has been deadened by the damper, the second chord sounding thereafter. Thus the change of pedal causes the dissonances to vanish; but, on the other hand, the change is so slight that one does not feel a change in the character of unpedalled or pedalled tones. Nor does the revival of the chord seem strange to the ear, since it is almost coincidental with the touch.

The ligature for chord progressions, also such which binds the successive diatonic and chromatic tone degrees, is completely solved by the syncopated mode of pedalling. In the case of slow chord progressions, one should tread the pedal precisely with the first chord touch and should only apply the syncopated pedal when the ensuing chord is struck. Countless examples of similar tone and chord connections can be found in music literature.

Pedal Application for Polyphonic Playing

The pedal can also be available in contrapuntal pieces and movements. Bach composed music for the pianos used in his time. The keys of those instruments were smaller and more narrow than those of the present piano. Therefore, it was possible to conjoin many notes without the aid of the pedal which would be impossible on the piano of today. In view of this, the pedal is a justifiable mechanical contrivance.

When pedalling fugues, discretion is necessary. For instance, in the playing of a Fugue, wherein an exact execution of four voices (or parts) is utterly necessary, the pedal must be used very discriminately. Incorrect application of the pedal may cause five or more notes to intermingle, which will be unsuitable in four-part settings. Therefore, in rendering a Fugue, the pedal should only be used for necessary ties which cannot be accomplished by the fingers alone. When using the pedal, short treads are sufficient. Herein, all repeated *legato* tones which I have already mentioned in the course of writing (and which are possible on the modern piano) belong to the same category.

Players who are unable to skilfully tread the pedals should play without them, although they will frequently be compelled to sacrifice an exact ligation in the carrying out of a motive.

Application of the Pedal for Extreme Finger Expansions (Transcriptions)

Two-part piano compositions have gone through an evolution in the course of time and have developed into expansive settings. The composers have become accustomed to transfer the many tone colors of the orchestra to the piano so that we can speak of an *orchestral piano setting.* We often come across long, sustained melody notes, sounding simultaneously with other figurations and melodic passages, as for instance, in "Vocal Transcriptions" by Liszt. Sometimes these compositions demand such extreme finger expansions that it is utterly impossible to hold certain melody tones *with the fingers.* Therefore the pedal must. aid in accomplishing these "holds."

Should any accumulation of dissonances ensue through such pedalling, they must be accepted as unavoidable, for the sake of the sustained melodic tones. As we have mentioned before, these ensuing dissonant tones will be absorbed by the harmony, thus leaving no bad impression. This orchestral piano setting, which is used abundantly by Schumann, Liszt, Brahms and modern composers, has also brought about many changes in the notation. Formerly composers would write note values which the fingers could sustain, but now the pedal is often indicated as a means of sustaining notes. It is self-evident that the pedal is always necessary in such emergencies and that it need not be indicated by a pedal signature. We refer to a fragment of Edv. Grieg's "To Spring."

Such "full-handed" playing now calls for the adaptive grace note "appoggiatura," which, above all, is very important as a harmonic fundamental tone. Since the grace note must sound into the adjacent chord, the pedal is again required to accomplish this feat. An example of this is: Hungarian Rhapsody, by Fr. Liszt, No. 14.

The pedal is very often applied as a "binding means" in transcriptions. When we play a vocal transcription, our main object should be the carrying out of the "singing tone" in so far as the melody is concerned. Naturally, the full value of each melody tone must be considered, particularly when both melody and accompaniment are played with one hand. The pedal will aid the player in the proper rendition of the aforesaid tones. Of course, here again it will be difficult to avoid the disturbing dissonances. For the sake of clear and exact rendition of the melody, we shall have to accept such musical flaws as are caused by pedalling. Liszt's Vocal Transcriptions are fine comparative examples.

3. Application of the Pedal to Express Characteristic Sound Differences

In order to predominantly express all characteristic sound differences, the pedal is used as follows:

(a) For single tones, which should predominate when played opposite to less important tones, and for tone progressions, which should be enlivened and colored through the supportable, resonant pedal tone.

(b) For sound groups, which should produce contrasted effects, as for example in Fantasy in f-minor, by Fr. Chopin, Op. 49.

Composers conceive "tone color of the pedal" as an enrichment of tone. It is intended for small parts and occasionally for complete compositions. The pedal tones appear to be surrounded by tone

137

vapor, which might be interrupted by a temporary prolongation of the pedal. The tread and release should be of short duration for immediate damper action. With this quick change the player often guards against a painful confusion of tones, but, on the other hand, he does not permit the tone vapor (which renders soft and somewhat blurred contours or outlines) to disappear. Out of this vapor the tones, when struck, will come forth as clear dots and lines, it all responding to the peculiarity of the piano tone, which rises brightly at the moment of touch and then expires quickly. This dying away of tones, in conjunction with the vibration of the untouched strings, distinguishes the so-called "tone vapor."

Differences in Sound of Unpedalled and Pedalled Tones

As we have already mentioned, the change of tone color in pedal tones, compared with unpedalled tones, is characteristic of the pedal effect. As we know, this alteration ensues through the simultaneous sounding of strings which are not struck by the hammers, and is dependent upon the octave position as well as the dynamical degree of touch. It is logical that a piece which is rendered with pedal will possess a different character of sound than the same piece which is performed without pedal; thus it means that the versatile artist will have to make the most of this difference.

First of all, this difference exists in the increase of sound which occasions the predominance of individual tones as well as complete tone groups.

The predominance of single tones, whether they are distinguished by a *sforzato* or by *fortepiano*, is attained through the effects of the pedal treads.

Simultaneous tone groups and consecutive arpeggios (broken chords) can unfold great splendor by means of effective pedalling; in fact, they can rise to rippling and roaring tone masses. Here the pedal is a necessary aid. It also furnishes relief to the player; in other words, it makes extreme dynamic intensification possible—from *piano* to *forte*, to *fff*.

Pedal Application for Tone Painting

The pedal is an essential auxiliary means in the attainment of tone painting. We shall use various examples to explain this.

Liszt wrote two Legends for piano: "Der heilige Franziskus, auf den Wogen schreitend," and "Die Vogelpredigt." In the first one Liszt portrays the rising and falling (swelling and breaking) of the waves by means of extended *ascending* and descending tone progressions which are partly chromatic. This "imitation of the roaring sea" demands pedalling throughout the said progressions, except at the end of the roll figures or where interruptions occur through very short pedal changes. In the "Vogelpredigt," the twittering and chirping of a swarm of birds is imitated by "tremolos," which properly float or blend into one another with the help of the pedal. Similar tone paintings (tempest, thunderstorm, rustling of

138

leaves, etc.) are frequent musical offerings, as for instance, in "Waldesrauschen" by Liszt and "The Linden Tree" by Schubert.

The prolongation of the pedal for complete parts of piano pieces with various harmonies (which has already been discussed), in opposition to the former drawn-up rules, can also occur by reason of tone painting.

In the final piece of the "Papillons," Robert Schumann writes twenty-six measures over the sustained bass-tone "d", these measures being played with a prolonged pedal. It is to be expected that in such cases foreign tones and harmonies intermingle, which do not sound very pleasant to the sensitive ear. As an independent number of "Papillons," this final piece would, therefore, create a bad impression upon the listeners. However, when this final piece is combined with the preceding ones, the last scene of the "Papillons" portrays a final, dreamlike "floating by" of the formerly described "Carnival Scenes." For that reason the prescribed repudiated pedalling can be represented esthetically and artistically.

As a conclusion of the brief views on pedalling, we shall give instructions on—

Pedal Application for Syncopes as a Means for Marking the Rhythm

Sonata in E-flat major (end of the exposition), by L. van Beethoven, Op. 7, 1st movement.

The carrying out of the syncopated notes in this Sonata is always recognized by the pedal tread on the heavy beat (first and fourth eighth-note). Most every pupil plays these *tied notes* (see above illustration) too shortly, thereby spoiling the character of the syncopes. The *tied chord*, even though it is not struck, becomes somewhat enlivened through the pedal tread on the *heavy beat*. In order to comprehend the syncope, it is important that the rhythm be observed and that the syncopated notes be held for their full value. The character of the syncope is recognized more easily, and the sustained note value is guaranteed through the "heavy-beat" pedal tread.

139

Using the Pedal for Trills

The quick succession of two seconds (vibration), which we term "trill," is the combining or blending of two adjacent notes. The intimate relation is especially achieved by means of the pedal. In my opinion, the trill should, therefore, be played with the pedal in most cases. Many pedagogues are of the opposite opinion, claiming that since two seconds produce a discord, the pedal should be avoided. However, this dissonance should appear as a *whole tone*. Of course, when playing chain trills (wherein the seconds continually change), we should tread and lift the pedal accordingly.

Using the Left Pedal

As we have already mentioned, the left pedal (also called the "*sordino* pedal") acts as a *sound diminisher*. In the so-called "pianettes" (or upright pianos) this mechanism works mostly in the following manner: The hammers are brought closer to the strings when the player treads on the left pedal. The strings, therefore, are struck with comparatively less force, since the hammer has less swing. The produced tone will, therefore, sound softer. This left pedal is used in certain places where an extreme "*piano*" is desirable. In grand pianos this left-pedal mechanism acts in the following manner: Every hammer is shifted when treading on this pedal so that only two of the three component strings (which are uniformly tuned for the production of one sound) are struck, or, as in our present grand piano, only *one* of the three strings is touched by the hammer. The down tread of the left pedal is indicated by the Italian designation "*una corda*" (one string), or occasionally, "*due corde*" (two strings). The designation "*tre corde*" (three strings) means that the foot should again be raised. Naturally, the damper is most effective when the hammer strikes only one string. It is obvious that the character of sound (referring to the grand piano) is somewhat influenced by the application of the left pedal. The tone easily becomes a trifle nasal and dull. This particular timbre (or tone color) is very often suggested by composers. On the other hand, the left pedal of the "pianette" only weakens the tone, but the character of sound remains unchanged. This contrivance of the "pianette" is not always reliable—not even in good instruments. Applying both pedals at the same time is very effective in many cases.

Many grand pianos have a third (*sostenuto*) pedal which serves as a prolonger of individual tones or chords.

A CATALOG OF SELECTED
DOVER BOOKS
IN ALL FIELDS OF INTEREST

A CATALOG OF SELECTED DOVER
BOOKS IN ALL FIELDS OF INTEREST

CONCERNING THE SPIRITUAL IN ART, Wassily Kandinsky. Pioneering work by father of abstract art. Thoughts on color theory, nature of art. Analysis of earlier masters. 12 illustrations. 80pp. of text. 5⅜ x 8½. 23411-8 Pa. $4.95

ANIMALS: 1,419 Copyright-Free Illustrations of Mammals, Birds, Fish, Insects, etc., Jim Harter (ed.). Clear wood engravings present, in extremely lifelike poses, over 1,000 species of animals. One of the most extensive pictorial sourcebooks of its kind. Captions. Index. 284pp. 9 x 12. 23766-4 Pa. $14.95

CELTIC ART: The Methods of Construction, George Bain. Simple geometric techniques for making Celtic interlacements, spirals, Kells-type initials, animals, humans, etc. Over 500 illustrations. 160pp. 9 x 12. (USO) 22923-8 Pa. $9.95

AN ATLAS OF ANATOMY FOR ARTISTS, Fritz Schider. Most thorough reference work on art anatomy in the world. Hundreds of illustrations, including selections from works by Vesalius, Leonardo, Goya, Ingres, Michelangelo, others. 593 illustrations. 192pp. 7⅛ x 10¼. 20241-0 Pa. $9.95

CELTIC HAND STROKE-BY-STROKE (Irish Half-Uncial from "The Book of Kells"): An Arthur Baker Calligraphy Manual, Arthur Baker. Complete guide to creating each letter of the alphabet in distinctive Celtic manner. Covers hand position, strokes, pens, inks, paper, more. Illustrated. 48pp. 8¼ x 11. 24336-2 Pa. $3.95

EASY ORIGAMI, John Montroll. Charming collection of 32 projects (hat, cup, pelican, piano, swan, many more) specially designed for the novice origami hobbyist. Clearly illustrated easy-to-follow instructions insure that even beginning papercrafters will achieve successful results. 48pp. 8¼ x 11. 27298-2 Pa. $3.50

THE COMPLETE BOOK OF BIRDHOUSE CONSTRUCTION FOR WOODWORKERS, Scott D. Campbell. Detailed instructions, illustrations, tables. Also data on bird habitat and instinct patterns. Bibliography. 3 tables. 63 illustrations in 15 figures. 48pp. 5¼ x 8½. 24407-5 Pa. $2.50

BLOOMINGDALE'S ILLUSTRATED 1886 CATALOG: Fashions, Dry Goods and Housewares, Bloomingdale Brothers. Famed merchants' extremely rare catalog depicting about 1,700 products: clothing, housewares, firearms, dry goods, jewelry, more. Invaluable for dating, identifying vintage items. Also, copyright-free graphics for artists, designers. Co-published with Henry Ford Museum & Greenfield Village. 160pp. 8¼ x 11. 25780-0 Pa. $10.95

HISTORIC COSTUME IN PICTURES, Braun & Schneider. Over 1,450 costumed figures in clearly detailed engravings–from dawn of civilization to end of 19th century. Captions. Many folk costumes. 256pp. 8⅜ x 11¾. 23150-X Pa. $12.95

CATALOG OF DOVER BOOKS

STICKLEY CRAFTSMAN FURNITURE CATALOGS, Gustav Stickley and L. & J. G. Stickley. Beautiful, functional furniture in two authentic catalogs from 1910. 594 illustrations, including 277 photos, show settles, rockers, armchairs, reclining chairs, bookcases, desks, tables. 183pp. 6½ x 9¼. 23838-5 Pa. $11.95

AMERICAN LOCOMOTIVES IN HISTORIC PHOTOGRAPHS: 1858 to 1949, Ron Ziel (ed.). A rare collection of 126 meticulously detailed official photographs, called "builder portraits," of American locomotives that majestically chronicle the rise of steam locomotive power in America. Introduction. Detailed captions. xi + 129pp. 9 x 12. 27393-8 Pa. $13.95

AMERICA'S LIGHTHOUSES: An Illustrated History, Francis Ross Holland, Jr. Delightfully written, profusely illustrated fact-filled survey of over 200 American lighthouses since 1716. History, anecdotes, technological advances, more. 240pp. 8 x 10¾. 25576-X Pa. $12.95

TOWARDS A NEW ARCHITECTURE, Le Corbusier. Pioneering manifesto by founder of "International School." Technical and aesthetic theories, views of industry, economics, relation of form to function, "mass-production split" and much more. Profusely illustrated. 320pp. 6⅛ x 9¼. (USO) 25023-7 Pa. $9.95

HOW THE OTHER HALF LIVES, Jacob Riis. Famous journalistic record, exposing poverty and degradation of New York slums around 1900, by major social reformer. 100 striking and influential photographs. 233pp. 10 x 7⅞. 22012-5 Pa. $11.95

FRUIT KEY AND TWIG KEY TO TREES AND SHRUBS, William M. Harlow. One of the handiest and most widely used identification aids. Fruit key covers 120 deciduous and evergreen species; twig key 160 deciduous species. Easily used. Over 300 photographs. 126pp. 5⅜ x 8½. 20511-8 Pa. $3.95

COMMON BIRD SONGS, Dr. Donald J. Borror. Songs of 60 most common U.S. birds: robins, sparrows, cardinals, bluejays, finches, more—arranged in order of increasing complexity. Up to 9 variations of songs of each species. Cassette and manual 99911-4 $8.95

ORCHIDS AS HOUSE PLANTS, Rebecca Tyson Northen. Grow cattleyas and many other kinds of orchids—in a window, in a case, or under artificial light. 63 illustrations. 148pp. 5⅜ x 8½. 23261-1 Pa. $5.95

MONSTER MAZES, Dave Phillips. Masterful mazes at four levels of difficulty. Avoid deadly perils and evil creatures to find magical treasures. Solutions for all 32 exciting illustrated puzzles. 48pp. 8¼ x 11. 26005-4 Pa. $2.95

MOZART'S DON GIOVANNI (DOVER OPERA LIBRETTO SERIES), Wolfgang Amadeus Mozart. Introduced and translated by Ellen H. Bleiler. Standard Italian libretto, with complete English translation. Convenient and thoroughly portable—an ideal companion for reading along with a recording or the performance itself. Introduction. List of characters. Plot summary. 121pp. 5¼ x 8½. 24944-1 Pa. $3.95

TECHNICAL MANUAL AND DICTIONARY OF CLASSICAL BALLET, Gail Grant. Defines, explains, comments on steps, movements, poses and concepts. 15-page pictorial section. Basic book for student, viewer. 127pp. 5⅜ x 8½. 21843-0 Pa. $4.95

BRASS INSTRUMENTS: Their History and Development, Anthony Baines. Authoritative, updated survey of the evolution of trumpets, trombones, bugles, cornets, French horns, tubas and other brass wind instruments. Over 140 illustrations and 48 music examples. Corrected and updated by author. New preface. Bibliography. 320pp. 5⅜ x 8½. 27574-4 Pa. $9.95

HOLLYWOOD GLAMOR PORTRAITS, John Kobal (ed.). 145 photos from 1926-49. Harlow, Gable, Bogart, Bacall; 94 stars in all. Full background on photographers, technical aspects. 160pp. 8⅜ x 11¼. 23352-9 Pa. $12.95

MAX AND MORITZ, Wilhelm Busch. Great humor classic in both German and English. Also 10 other works: "Cat and Mouse," "Plisch and Plumm," etc. 216pp. 5⅜ x 8½. 20181-3 Pa. $6.95

THE RAVEN AND OTHER FAVORITE POEMS, Edgar Allan Poe. Over 40 of the author's most memorable poems: "The Bells," "Ulalume," "Israfel," "To Helen," "The Conqueror Worm," "Eldorado," "Annabel Lee," many more. Alphabetic lists of titles and first lines. 64pp. 5$\frac{3}{16}$ x 8¼. 26685-0 Pa. $1.00

PERSONAL MEMOIRS OF U. S. GRANT, Ulysses Simpson Grant. Intelligent, deeply moving firsthand account of Civil War campaigns, considered by many the finest military memoirs ever written. Includes letters, historic photographs, maps and more. 528pp. 6⅛ x 9¼. 28587-1 Pa. $12.95

AMULETS AND SUPERSTITIONS, E. A. Wallis Budge. Comprehensive discourse on origin, powers of amulets in many ancient cultures: Arab, Persian Babylonian, Assyrian, Egyptian, Gnostic, Hebrew, Phoenician, Syriac, etc. Covers cross, swastika, crucifix, seals, rings, stones, etc. 584pp. 5⅜ x 8½. 23573-4 Pa. $15.95

RUSSIAN STORIES/PYCCKNE PACCKA3bl: A Dual-Language Book, edited by Gleb Struve. Twelve tales by such masters as Chekhov, Tolstoy, Dostoevsky, Pushkin, others. Excellent word-for-word English translations on facing pages, plus teaching and study aids, Russian/English vocabulary, biographical/critical introductions, more. 416pp. 5⅜ x 8½. 26244-8 Pa. $9.95

PHILADELPHIA THEN AND NOW: 60 Sites Photographed in the Past and Present, Kenneth Finkel and Susan Oyama. Rare photographs of City Hall, Logan Square, Independence Hall, Betsy Ross House, other landmarks juxtaposed with contemporary views. Captures changing face of historic city. Introduction. Captions. 128pp. 8¼ x 11. 25790-8 Pa. $9.95

AIA ARCHITECTURAL GUIDE TO NASSAU AND SUFFOLK COUNTIES, LONG ISLAND, The American Institute of Architects, Long Island Chapter, and the Society for the Preservation of Long Island Antiquities. Comprehensive, well-researched and generously illustrated volume brings to life over three centuries of Long Island's great architectural heritage. More than 240 photographs with authoritative, extensively detailed captions. 176pp. 8¼ x 11. 26946-9 Pa. $14.95

NORTH AMERICAN INDIAN LIFE: Customs and Traditions of 23 Tribes, Elsie Clews Parsons (ed.). 27 fictionalized essays by noted anthropologists examine religion, customs, government, additional facets of life among the Winnebago, Crow, Zuni, Eskimo, other tribes. 480pp. 6⅛ x 9¼. 27377-6 Pa. $10.95

ANATOMY: A Complete Guide for Artists, Joseph Sheppard. A master of figure drawing shows artists how to render human anatomy convincingly. Over 460 illustrations. 224pp. 8⅜ x 11¼. 27279-6 Pa. $11.95

MEDIEVAL CALLIGRAPHY: Its History and Technique, Marc Drogin. Spirited history, comprehensive instruction manual covers 13 styles (ca. 4th century thru 15th). Excellent photographs; directions for duplicating medieval techniques with modern tools. 224pp. 8⅜ x 11¼. 26142-5 Pa. $12.95

DRIED FLOWERS: How to Prepare Them, Sarah Whitlock and Martha Rankin. Complete instructions on how to use silica gel, meal and borax, perlite aggregate, sand and borax, glycerine and water to create attractive permanent flower arrangements. 12 illustrations. 32pp. 5⅜ x 8½. 21802-3 Pa. $1.00

EASY-TO-MAKE BIRD FEEDERS FOR WOODWORKERS, Scott D. Campbell. Detailed, simple-to-use guide for designing, constructing, caring for and using feeders. Text, illustrations for 12 classic and contemporary designs. 96pp. 5⅜ x 8½. 25847-5 Pa. $3.95

SCOTTISH WONDER TALES FROM MYTH AND LEGEND, Donald A. Mackenzie. 16 lively tales tell of giants rumbling down mountainsides, of a magic wand that turns stone pillars into warriors, of gods and goddesses, evil hags, powerful forces and more. 240pp. 5⅜ x 8½. 29677-6 Pa. $6.95

THE HISTORY OF UNDERCLOTHES, C. Willett Cunnington and Phyllis Cunnington. Fascinating, well-documented survey covering six centuries of English undergarments, enhanced with over 100 illustrations: 12th-century laced-up bodice, footed long drawers (1795), 19th-century bustles, 19th-century corsets for men, Victorian "bust improvers," much more. 272pp. 5⅝ x 8¼. 27124-2 Pa. $9.95

ARTS AND CRAFTS FURNITURE: The Complete Brooks Catalog of 1912, Brooks Manufacturing Co. Photos and detailed descriptions of more than 150 now very collectible furniture designs from the Arts and Crafts movement depict davenports, settees, buffets, desks, tables, chairs, bedsteads, dressers and more, all built of solid, quarter-sawed oak. Invaluable for students and enthusiasts of antiques, Americana and the decorative arts. 80pp. 6½ x 9¼. 27471-3 Pa. $8.95

HOW WE INVENTED THE AIRPLANE: An Illustrated History, Orville Wright. Fascinating firsthand account covers early experiments, construction of planes and motors, first flights, much more. Introduction and commentary by Fred C. Kelly. 76 photographs. 96pp. 8¼ x 11. 25662-6 Pa. $8.95

THE ARTS OF THE SAILOR: Knotting, Splicing and Ropework, Hervey Garrett Smith. Indispensable shipboard reference covers tools, basic knots and useful hitches; handsewing and canvas work, more. Over 100 illustrations. Delightful reading for sea lovers. 256pp. 5⅜ x 8½. 26440-8 Pa. $8.95

FRANK LLOYD WRIGHT'S FALLINGWATER: The House and Its History, Second, Revised Edition, Donald Hoffmann. A total revision–both in text and illustrations–of the standard document on Fallingwater, the boldest, most personal architectural statement of Wright's mature years, updated with valuable new material from the recently opened Frank Lloyd Wright Archives. "Fascinating"–*The New York Times.* 116 illustrations. 128pp. 9¼ x 10¾. 27430-6 Pa. $12.95

THE BEST TALES OF HOFFMANN, E. T. A. Hoffmann. 10 of Hoffmann's most important stories: "Nutcracker and the King of Mice," "The Golden Flowerpot," etc. 458pp. 5⅜ x 8½. 21793-0 Pa. $9.95

FROM FETISH TO GOD IN ANCIENT EGYPT, E. A. Wallis Budge. Rich detailed survey of Egyptian conception of "God" and gods, magic, cult of animals, Osiris, more. Also, superb English translations of hymns and legends. 240 illustrations. 545pp. 5⅜ x 8½. 25803-3 Pa. $13.95

FRENCH STORIES/CONTES FRANÇAIS: A Dual-Language Book, Wallace Fowlie. Ten stories by French masters, Voltaire to Camus: "Micromegas" by Voltaire; "The Atheist's Mass" by Balzac; "Minuet" by de Maupassant; "The Guest" by Camus, six more. Excellent English translations on facing pages. Also French-English vocabulary list, exercises, more. 352pp. 5⅜ x 8½. 26443-2 Pa. $9.95

CHICAGO AT THE TURN OF THE CENTURY IN PHOTOGRAPHS: 122 Historic Views from the Collections of the Chicago Historical Society, Larry A. Viskochil. Rare large-format prints offer detailed views of City Hall, State Street, the Loop, Hull House, Union Station, many other landmarks, circa 1904-1913. Introduction. Captions. Maps. 144pp. 9⅜ x 12¼. 24656-6 Pa. $12.95

OLD BROOKLYN IN EARLY PHOTOGRAPHS, 1865-1929, William Lee Younger. Luna Park, Gravesend race track, construction of Grand Army Plaza, moving of Hotel Brighton, etc. 157 previously unpublished photographs. 165pp. 8⅞ x 11¾. 23587-4 Pa. $13.95

THE MYTHS OF THE NORTH AMERICAN INDIANS, Lewis Spence. Rich anthology of the myths and legends of the Algonquins, Iroquois, Pawnees and Sioux, prefaced by an extensive historical and ethnological commentary. 36 illustrations. 480pp. 5⅜ x 8½. 25967-6 Pa. $10.95

AN ENCYCLOPEDIA OF BATTLES: Accounts of Over 1,560 Battles from 1479 B.C. to the Present, David Eggenberger. Essential details of every major battle in recorded history from the first battle of Megiddo in 1479 B.C. to Grenada in 1984. List of Battle Maps. New Appendix covering the years 1967-1984. Index. 99 illustrations. 544pp. 6½ x 9¼. 24913-1 Pa. $16.95

SAILING ALONE AROUND THE WORLD, Captain Joshua Slocum. First man to sail around the world, alone, in small boat. One of great feats of seamanship told in delightful manner. 67 illustrations. 294pp. 5⅜ x 8½. 20326-3 Pa. $6.95

ANARCHISM AND OTHER ESSAYS, Emma Goldman. Powerful, penetrating, prophetic essays on direct action, role of minorities, prison reform, puritan hypocrisy, violence, etc. 271pp. 5⅜ x 8½. 22484-8 Pa. $7.95

MYTHS OF THE HINDUS AND BUDDHISTS, Ananda K. Coomaraswamy and Sister Nivedita. Great stories of the epics; deeds of Krishna, Shiva, taken from puranas, Vedas, folk tales; etc. 32 illustrations. 400pp. 5⅜ x 8½. 21759-0 Pa. $12.95

BEYOND PSYCHOLOGY, Otto Rank. Fear of death, desire of immortality, nature of sexuality, social organization, creativity, according to Rankian system. 291pp. 5⅜ x 8½. 20485-5 Pa. $8.95

A THEOLOGICO-POLITICAL TREATISE, Benedict Spinoza. Also contains unfinished Political Treatise. Great classic on religious liberty, theory of government on common consent. R. Elwes translation. Total of 421pp. 5⅜ x 8½. 20249-6 Pa. $9.95

CATALOG OF DOVER BOOKS

MY BONDAGE AND MY FREEDOM, Frederick Douglass. Born a slave, Douglass became outspoken force in antislavery movement. The best of Douglass' autobiographies. Graphic description of slave life. 464pp. 5⅜ x 8½. 22457-0 Pa. $8.95

FOLLOWING THE EQUATOR: A Journey Around the World, Mark Twain. Fascinating humorous account of 1897 voyage to Hawaii, Australia, India, New Zealand, etc. Ironic, bemused reports on peoples, customs, climate, flora and fauna, politics, much more. 197 illustrations. 720pp. 5⅜ x 8½. 26113-1 Pa. $15.95

THE PEOPLE CALLED SHAKERS, Edward D. Andrews. Definitive study of Shakers: origins, beliefs, practices, dances, social organization, furniture and crafts, etc. 33 illustrations. 351pp. 5⅜ x 8½. 21081-2 Pa. $8.95

THE MYTHS OF GREECE AND ROME, H. A. Guerber. A classic of mythology, generously illustrated, long prized for its simple, graphic, accurate retelling of the principal myths of Greece and Rome, and for its commentary on their origins and significance. With 64 illustrations by Michelangelo, Raphael, Titian, Rubens, Canova, Bernini and others. 480pp. 5⅜ x 8½. 27584-1 Pa. $9.95

PSYCHOLOGY OF MUSIC, Carl E. Seashore. Classic work discusses music as a medium from psychological viewpoint. Clear treatment of physical acoustics, auditory apparatus, sound perception, development of musical skills, nature of musical feeling, host of other topics. 88 figures. 408pp. 5⅜ x 8½. 21851-1 Pa. $11.95

THE PHILOSOPHY OF HISTORY, Georg W. Hegel. Great classic of Western thought develops concept that history is not chance but rational process, the evolution of freedom. 457pp. 5⅜ x 8½. 20112-0 Pa. $9.95

THE BOOK OF TEA, Kakuzo Okakura. Minor classic of the Orient: entertaining, charming explanation, interpretation of traditional Japanese culture in terms of tea ceremony. 94pp. 5⅜ x 8½. 20070-1 Pa. $3.95

LIFE IN ANCIENT EGYPT, Adolf Erman. Fullest, most thorough, detailed older account with much not in more recent books, domestic life, religion, magic, medicine, commerce, much more. Many illustrations reproduce tomb paintings, carvings, hieroglyphs, etc. 597pp. 5⅜ x 8½. 22632-8 Pa. $12.95

SUNDIALS, Their Theory and Construction, Albert Waugh. Far and away the best, most thorough coverage of ideas, mathematics concerned, types, construction, adjusting anywhere. Simple, nontechnical treatment allows even children to build several of these dials. Over 100 illustrations. 230pp. 5⅜ x 8½. 22947-5 Pa. $8.95

DYNAMICS OF FLUIDS IN POROUS MEDIA, Jacob Bear. For advanced students of ground water hydrology, soil mechanics and physics, drainage and irrigation engineering, and more. 335 illustrations. Exercises, with answers. 784pp. 6⅛ x 9¼. 65675-6 Pa. $19.95

SONGS OF EXPERIENCE: Facsimile Reproduction with 26 Plates in Full Color, William Blake. 26 full-color plates from a rare 1826 edition. Includes "TheTyger," "London," "Holy Thursday," and other poems. Printed text of poems. 48pp. 5¼ x 7. 24636-1 Pa. $4.95

OLD-TIME VIGNETTES IN FULL COLOR, Carol Belanger Grafton (ed.). Over 390 charming, often sentimental illustrations, selected from archives of Victorian graphics—pretty women posing, children playing, food, flowers, kittens and puppies, smiling cherubs, birds and butterflies, much more. All copyright-free. 48pp. 9¼ x 12¼. 27269-9 Pa. $7.95

PERSPECTIVE FOR ARTISTS, Rex Vicat Cole. Depth, perspective of sky and sea, shadows, much more, not usually covered. 391 diagrams, 81 reproductions of drawings and paintings. 279pp. 5⅜ x 8½. 22487-2 Pa. $7.95

DRAWING THE LIVING FIGURE, Joseph Sheppard. Innovative approach to artistic anatomy focuses on specifics of surface anatomy, rather than muscles and bones. Over 170 drawings of live models in front, back and side views, and in widely varying poses. Accompanying diagrams. 177 illustrations. Introduction. Index. 144pp. 8⅜ x11¼. 26723-7 Pa. $8.95

GOTHIC AND OLD ENGLISH ALPHABETS: 100 Complete Fonts, Dan X. Solo. Add power, elegance to posters, signs, other graphics with 100 stunning copyright-free alphabets: Blackstone, Dolbey, Germania, 97 more–including many lower-case, numerals, punctuation marks. 104pp. 8⅛ x 11. 24695-7 Pa. $8.95

HOW TO DO BEADWORK, Mary White. Fundamental book on craft from simple projects to five-bead chains and woven works. 106 illustrations. 142pp. 5⅜ x 8. 20697-1 Pa. $5.95

THE BOOK OF WOOD CARVING, Charles Marshall Sayers. Finest book for beginners discusses fundamentals and offers 34 designs. "Absolutely first rate . . . well thought out and well executed."–E. J. Tangerman. 118pp. 7¾ x 10⅝. 23654-4 Pa. $7.95

ILLUSTRATED CATALOG OF CIVIL WAR MILITARY GOODS: Union Army Weapons, Insignia, Uniform Accessories, and Other Equipment, Schuyler, Hartley, and Graham. Rare, profusely illustrated 1846 catalog includes Union Army uniform and dress regulations, arms and ammunition, coats, insignia, flags, swords, rifles, etc. 226 illustrations. 160pp. 9 x 12. 24939-5 Pa. $10.95

WOMEN'S FASHIONS OF THE EARLY 1900s: An Unabridged Republication of "New York Fashions, 1909," National Cloak & Suit Co. Rare catalog of mail-order fashions documents women's and children's clothing styles shortly after the turn of the century. Captions offer full descriptions, prices. Invaluable resource for fashion, costume historians. Approximately 725 illustrations. 128pp. 8⅜ x 11¼. 27276-1 Pa. $11.95

THE 1912 AND 1915 GUSTAV STICKLEY FURNITURE CATALOGS, Gustav Stickley. With over 200 detailed illustrations and descriptions, these two catalogs are essential reading and reference materials and identification guides for Stickley furniture. Captions cite materials, dimensions and prices. 112pp. 6½ x 9¼. 26676-1 Pa. $9.95

EARLY AMERICAN LOCOMOTIVES, John H. White, Jr. Finest locomotive engravings from early 19th century: historical (1804–74), main-line (after 1870), special, foreign, etc. 147 plates. 142pp. 11⅜ x 8¼. 22772-3 Pa. $10.95

THE TALL SHIPS OF TODAY IN PHOTOGRAPHS, Frank O. Braynard. Lavishly illustrated tribute to nearly 100 majestic contemporary sailing vessels: Amerigo Vespucci, Clearwater, Constitution, Eagle, Mayflower, Sea Cloud, Victory, many more. Authoritative captions provide statistics, background on each ship. 190 black-and-white photographs and illustrations. Introduction. 128pp. 8⅞ x 11¾. 27163-3 Pa. $14.95

FRANK LLOYD WRIGHT'S HOLLYHOCK HOUSE, Donald Hoffmann. Lavishly illustrated, carefully documented study of one of Wright's most controversial residential designs. Over 120 photographs, floor plans, elevations, etc. Detailed perceptive text by noted Wright scholar. Index. 128pp. 9¼ x 10¾. 27133-1 Pa. $11.95

THE MALE AND FEMALE FIGURE IN MOTION: 60 Classic Photographic Sequences, Eadweard Muybridge. 60 true-action photographs of men and women walking, running, climbing, bending, turning, etc., reproduced from rare 19th-century masterpiece. vi + 121pp. 9 x 12. 24745-7 Pa. $10.95

1001 QUESTIONS ANSWERED ABOUT THE SEASHORE, N. J. Berrill and Jacquelyn Berrill. Queries answered about dolphins, sea snails, sponges, starfish, fishes, shore birds, many others. Covers appearance, breeding, growth, feeding, much more. 305pp. 5¼ x 8¼. 23366-9 Pa. $9.95

GUIDE TO OWL WATCHING IN NORTH AMERICA, Donald S. Heintzelman. Superb guide offers complete data and descriptions of 19 species: barn owl, screech owl, snowy owl, many more. Expert coverage of owl-watching equipment, conservation, migrations and invasions, etc. Guide to observing sites. 84 illustrations. xiii + 193pp. 5⅜ x 8½. 27344-X Pa. $8.95

MEDICINAL AND OTHER USES OF NORTH AMERICAN PLANTS: A Historical Survey with Special Reference to the Eastern Indian Tribes, Charlotte Erichsen-Brown. Chronological historical citations document 500 years of usage of plants, trees, shrubs native to eastern Canada, northeastern U.S. Also complete identifying information. 343 illustrations. 544pp. 6½ x 9¼. 25951-X Pa. $12.95

STORYBOOK MAZES, Dave Phillips. 23 stories and mazes on two-page spreads: Wizard of Oz, Treasure Island, Robin Hood, etc. Solutions. 64pp. 8¼ x 11. 23628-5 Pa. $2.95

NEGRO FOLK MUSIC, U.S.A., Harold Courlander. Noted folklorist's scholarly yet readable analysis of rich and varied musical tradition. Includes authentic versions of over 40 folk songs. Valuable bibliography and discography. xi + 324pp. 5⅜ x 8½. 27350-4 Pa. $9.95

MOVIE-STAR PORTRAITS OF THE FORTIES, John Kobal (ed.). 163 glamor, studio photos of 106 stars of the 1940s: Rita Hayworth, Ava Gardner, Marlon Brando, Clark Gable, many more. 176pp. 8⅜ x 11¼. 23546-7 Pa. $14.95

BENCHLEY LOST AND FOUND, Robert Benchley. Finest humor from early 30s, about pet peeves, child psychologists, post office and others. Mostly unavailable elsewhere. 73 illustrations by Peter Arno and others. 183pp. 5⅜ x 8½. 22410-4 Pa. $6.95

YEKL and THE IMPORTED BRIDEGROOM AND OTHER STORIES OF YIDDISH NEW YORK, Abraham Cahan. Film Hester Street based on Yekl (1896). Novel, other stories among first about Jewish immigrants on N.Y.'s East Side. 240pp. 5⅜ x 8½. 22427-9 Pa. $6.95

SELECTED POEMS, Walt Whitman. Generous sampling from *Leaves of Grass*. Twenty-four poems include "I Hear America Singing," "Song of the Open Road," "I Sing the Body Electric," "When Lilacs Last in the Dooryard Bloom'd," "O Captain! My Captain!"—all reprinted from an authoritative edition. Lists of titles and first lines. 128pp. 5³⁄₁₆ x 8¼. 26878-0 Pa. $1.00

PIANO TUNING, J. Cree Fischer. Clearest, best book for beginner, amateur. Simple repairs, raising dropped notes, tuning by easy method of flattened fifths. No previous skills needed. 4 illustrations. 201pp. 5⅜ x 8½. 23267-0 Pa. $6.95

A SOURCE BOOK IN THEATRICAL HISTORY, A. M. Nagler. Contemporary observers on acting, directing, make-up, costuming, stage props, machinery, scene design, from Ancient Greece to Chekhov. 611pp. 5⅜ x 8½. 20515-0 Pa. $12.95

THE COMPLETE NONSENSE OF EDWARD LEAR, Edward Lear. All nonsense limericks, zany alphabets, Owl and Pussycat, songs, nonsense botany, etc., illustrated by Lear. Total of 320pp. 5⅜ x 8½. (USO) 20167-8 Pa. $7.95

VICTORIAN PARLOUR POETRY: An Annotated Anthology, Michael R. Turner. 117 gems by Longfellow, Tennyson, Browning, many lesser-known poets. "The Village Blacksmith," "Curfew Must Not Ring Tonight," "Only a Baby Small," dozens more, often difficult to find elsewhere. Index of poets, titles, first lines. xxiii + 325pp. 5⅝ x 8¼. 27044-0 Pa. $8.95

DUBLINERS, James Joyce. Fifteen stories offer vivid, tightly focused observations of the lives of Dublin's poorer classes. At least one, "The Dead," is considered a masterpiece. Reprinted complete and unabridged from standard edition. 160pp. 5³⁄₁₆ x 8¼. 26870-5 Pa. $1.00

THE HAUNTED MONASTERY and THE CHINESE MAZE MURDERS, Robert van Gulik. Two full novels by van Gulik, set in 7th-century China, continue adventures of Judge Dee and his companions. An evil Taoist monastery, seemingly supernatural events; overgrown topiary maze hides strange crimes. 27 illustrations. 328pp. 5⅜ x 8½. 23502-5 Pa. $8.95

THE BOOK OF THE SACRED MAGIC OF ABRAMELIN THE MAGE, translated by S. MacGregor Mathers. Medieval manuscript of ceremonial magic. Basic document in Aleister Crowley, Golden Dawn groups. 268pp. 5⅜ x 8½. 23211-5 Pa. $9.95

NEW RUSSIAN-ENGLISH AND ENGLISH-RUSSIAN DICTIONARY, M. A. O'Brien. This is a remarkably handy Russian dictionary, containing a surprising amount of information, including over 70,000 entries. 366pp. 4½ x 6⅛. 20208-9 Pa. $10.95

HISTORIC HOMES OF THE AMERICAN PRESIDENTS, Second, Revised Edition, Irvin Haas. A traveler's guide to American Presidential homes, most open to the public, depicting and describing homes occupied by every American President from George Washington to George Bush. With visiting hours, admission charges, travel routes. 175 photographs. Index. 160pp. 8¼ x 11. 26751-2 Pa. $11.95

NEW YORK IN THE FORTIES, Andreas Feininger. 162 brilliant photographs by the well-known photographer, formerly with *Life* magazine. Commuters, shoppers, Times Square at night, much else from city at its peak. Captions by John von Hartz. 181pp. 9¼ x 10¾. 23585-8 Pa. $13.95

INDIAN SIGN LANGUAGE, William Tomkins. Over 525 signs developed by Sioux and other tribes. Written instructions and diagrams. Also 290 pictographs. 111pp. 6⅛ x 9¼. 22029-X Pa. $3.95

THE INFLUENCE OF SEA POWER UPON HISTORY, 1660–1783, A. T. Mahan. Influential classic of naval history and tactics still used as text in war colleges. First paperback edition. 4 maps. 24 battle plans. 640pp. 5⅜ x 8½. 25509-3 Pa. $14.95

THE STORY OF THE TITANIC AS TOLD BY ITS SURVIVORS, Jack Winocour (ed.). What it was really like. Panic, despair, shocking inefficiency, and a little heroism. More thrilling than any fictional account. 26 illustrations. 320pp. 5⅜ x 8½. 20610-6 Pa. $8.95

FAIRY AND FOLK TALES OF THE IRISH PEASANTRY, William Butler Yeats (ed.). Treasury of 64 tales from the twilight world of Celtic myth and legend: "The Soul Cages," "The Kildare Pooka," "King O'Toole and his Goose," many more. Introduction and Notes by W. B. Yeats. 352pp. 5⅜ x 8½. 26941-8 Pa. $8.95

BUDDHIST MAHAYANA TEXTS, E. B. Cowell and Others (eds.). Superb, accurate translations of basic documents in Mahayana Buddhism, highly important in history of religions. The Buddha-karita of Asvaghosha, Larger Sukhavativyuha, more. 448pp. 5⅜ x 8½. 25552-2 Pa. $12.95

ONE TWO THREE . . . INFINITY: Facts and Speculations of Science, George Gamow. Great physicist's fascinating, readable overview of contemporary science: number theory, relativity, fourth dimension, entropy, genes, atomic structure, much more. 128 illustrations. Index. 352pp. 5⅜ x 8½. 25664-2 Pa. $8.95

ENGINEERING IN HISTORY, Richard Shelton Kirby, et al. Broad, nontechnical survey of history's major technological advances: birth of Greek science, industrial revolution, electricity and applied science, 20th-century automation, much more. 181 illustrations. ". . . excellent . . ."–*Isis.* Bibliography. vii + 530pp. 5⅜ x 8¼. 26412-2 Pa. $14.95

DALÍ ON MODERN ART: The Cuckolds of Antiquated Modern Art, Salvador Dalí. Influential painter skewers modern art and its practitioners. Outrageous evaluations of Picasso, Cézanne, Turner, more. 15 renderings of paintings discussed. 44 calligraphic decorations by Dalí. 96pp. 5⅜ x 8½. (USO) 29220-7 Pa. $4.95

ANTIQUE PLAYING CARDS: A Pictorial History, Henry René D'Allemagne. Over 900 elaborate, decorative images from rare playing cards (14th–20th centuries): Bacchus, death, dancing dogs, hunting scenes, royal coats of arms, players cheating, much more. 96pp. 9¼ x 12¼. 29265-7 Pa. $12.95

MAKING FURNITURE MASTERPIECES: 30 Projects with Measured Drawings, Franklin H. Gottshall. Step-by-step instructions, illustrations for constructing handsome, useful pieces, among them a Sheraton desk, Chippendale chair, Spanish desk, Queen Anne table and a William and Mary dressing mirror. 224pp. 8⅛ x 11¼. 29338-6 Pa. $13.95

THE FOSSIL BOOK: A Record of Prehistoric Life, Patricia V. Rich et al. Profusely illustrated definitive guide covers everything from single-celled organisms and dinosaurs to birds and mammals and the interplay between climate and man. Over 1,500 illustrations. 760pp. 7½ x 10⅛. 29371-8 Pa. $29.95

Prices subject to change without notice.

Available at your book dealer or write for free catalog to Dept. GI, Dover Publications, Inc., 31 East 2nd St., Mineola, N.Y. 11501. Dover publishes more than 500 books each year on science, elementary and advanced mathematics, biology, music, art, literary history, social sciences and other areas.